ADOBE® CREATIVE SUITE® 5
DESIGN PREMIUM
CLASSROOM IN A BOOK®

The official training workbook from Adobe Systems

www.adobepress.com

Adobe

Writer: Conrad Chavez

Project Editor: Susan Rimerman

Production Editor: Tracey Croom

Development/Copyeditor: Anne Marie Walker

Technical Editor: Jean-Claude Tremblay

Proofer: Liz Avery Merfeld

Compositor: Lisa Fridsma

Indexer: Rebecca Plunkett

Cover design: Eddie Yuen

Interior design: Mimi Heft

WHAT'S ON THE DISC

Here is an overview of the contents of the Classroom in a Book disc

The *Adobe Creative Suite 5 Design Premium Classroom in a Book* disc includes the lesson files that you'll need to complete the exercises in this book, as well as other content to help you learn more about Adobe Creative Suite 5 and use it with greater efficiency and ease. The diagram below represents the contents of the disc, which should help you locate the files you need.

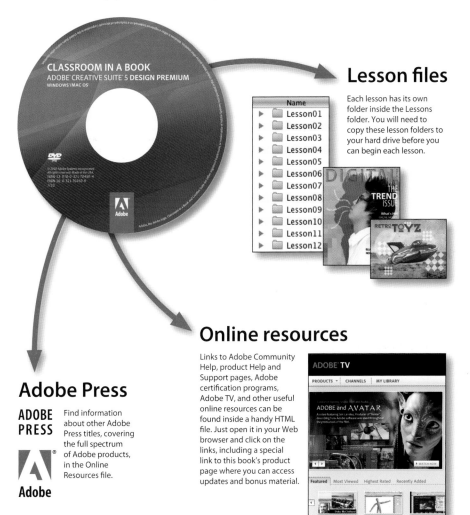

Lesson files

Each lesson has its own folder inside the Lessons folder. You will need to copy these lesson folders to your hard drive before you can begin each lesson.

Online resources

Links to Adobe Community Help, product Help and Support pages, Adobe certification programs, Adobe TV, and other useful online resources can be found inside a handy HTML file. Just open it in your Web browser and click on the links, including a special link to this book's product page where you can access updates and bonus material.

Adobe Press

Find information about other Adobe Press titles, covering the full spectrum of Adobe products, in the Online Resources file.

CONTENTS

GETTING STARTED

Adobe Creative Suite 5 is a unified design environment that delivers the next level of integration in creative software. Discover powerful new creative tools for expressing your ideas and crafting artwork that stands out. Finish your work faster with numerous enhancements to the tools you use every day. Extend the reach of your designs to new media without writing code. Streamline creative reviews and other essential but time-consuming tasks.

This Classroom in a Book introduces you to the key elements and applications of Adobe Creative Suite 5 Design Premium.

About Classroom in a Book

Adobe Creative Suite 5 Design Premium Classroom in a Book is part of the official training series for Adobe graphics and publishing software developed with the support of Adobe product experts. Each lesson in this book is made up of a series of self-paced projects that give you hands-on experience using the following Adobe products: Adobe InDesign CS5, Adobe Photoshop CS5 Extended, Adobe Illustrator CS5, Adobe Flash CS5 Professional, Adobe Dreamweaver CS5, Fireworks CS5, Adobe Flash Catalyst CS5, Adobe Acrobat 9 Pro, Adobe Device Central CS5, Adobe Media Encoder, and Adobe Bridge CS5.

Adobe Creative Suite 5 Design Premium Classroom in a Book includes a disc attached to the inside back cover. On the disc you'll find all the files used for the lessons in this book along with additional learning resources.

Prerequisites

Before you begin working on the lessons in this book, make sure that you and your computer are ready.

Computer requirements

You'll need about 1GB of free space on your hard disk to store all of the lesson files and the work files that you'll create as you work through the exercises. You'll need less space if don't store all of the lesson folders on your hard disk at once.

Required skills

The lessons in this book assume that you have a working knowledge of your computer and its operating system. Make sure that you know how to use the pointer and the standard menus and commands, and also how to open, save, and close files. Do you know how to use context menus, which open when you right-click/ Control-click items? Can you scroll (vertically and horizontally) within a window to see contents that may not be visible in the displayed area?

If you need to review these basic and generic computer skills, see the documentation included with your Microsoft Windows or Apple Mac OS X software.

Installing Adobe Creative Suite 5 Design Premium

Before you begin using *Adobe Creative Suite 5 Design Premium Classroom in a Book*, make sure that your system is set up correctly and that you've installed the required software and hardware. You must purchase the Adobe Creative Suite 5 Design Premium software separately. For system requirements and complete instructions on installing the software, see the Adobe Creative Suite 5 Design Premium Read Me file on the application installation disc or the Adobe Creative Suite Support Center on the web at www.adobe.com/support/creativesuite.

Make sure that your serial number is accessible before installing the software; you can find the serial number on the registration card or disc sleeve. For software you downloaded as an electronic purchase directly from Adobe, look for your serial number in the order confirmation e-mail and in your Adobe Store account on Adobe.com.

Copying the Classroom in a Book files

The disc attached to the inside back cover of this book includes a Lessons folder containing all the files you'll need for the lessons. Each lesson has its own folder; you must copy the folders to your hard disk to complete the lessons. To save room on your hard disk, you can copy only the folder necessary for each lesson as you need it, and remove it when you're done.

Copying the Lessons files from the disc

1   Insert the *Adobe Creative Suite 5 Design Premium Classroom in a Book* disc into your optical disc drive.

2   Browse the contents and locate the Lessons folder.

3   Do one of the following:

- To copy all the lesson files, drag the Lessons folder from the disc onto your hard disk.

- To copy only individual lesson files, first create a new folder on your hard disk and name it Lessons. Then drag the lesson folder or folders that you want to copy from the disc into the Lessons folder on your hard disk.

4   When your computer has finished copying the files, remove the disc from your optical disc drive and put it away.

Additional resources

Adobe Creative Suite 5 Design Premium CS5 Classroom in a Book is not meant to replace documentation that comes with the program or to be a comprehensive reference for every feature. Only the commands and options used in the lessons are explained in this book. For comprehensive information about program features and tutorials, refer to these resources:

Adobe Community Help: Community Help brings together active Adobe product users, Adobe product team members, authors, and experts to give you the most useful, relevant, and up-to-date information about Adobe products. Whether you're looking for a code sample or an answer to a problem, have a question about the software, or want to share a useful tip or recipe, you'll benefit from Community Help. Search results will show you not only content from Adobe, but also from the community.

● **Note:** The files on the disc are practice files, provided for your personal use in these lessons. You are not authorized to use these files commercially or to publish or distribute them in any form without written permission from Adobe Systems, Inc., and the individual photographers who took the pictures, or other copyright holders.

With Adobe Community Help you can:

- Access up-to-date definitive reference content online and offline
- Find the most relevant content contributed by experts from the Adobe community, on and off Adobe.com
- Comment on, rate, and contribute to content in the Adobe community
- Download Help content directly to your desktop for offline use
- Find related content with dynamic search and navigation tools

To access Community Help: If you have any Adobe CS5 product, then you already have the Community Help application. To invoke Help, **choose Help > [*Application name*] Help**. (For example in Dreamwever, choose Help > Dreamweaver Help. This companion application lets you search and browse Adobe and community content, plus you can comment on and rate any article just like you would in the browser. However, you can also download Adobe Help and language reference content for use offline. You can also subscribe to new content updates (which can be automatically downloaded) so that you'll always have the most up-to-date content for your Adobe product at all times. You can download the application from www.adobe.com/support/chc/index.html.

Adobe content is updated based on community feedback and contributions. You can contribute in several ways: add comments to content or forums, including links to web content; publish your own content using Community Publishing; or contribute Cookbook Recipes. Find out how to contribute: www.adobe.com/community/publishing/download.html .

See http://community.adobe.com/help/profile/faq.html for answers to frequently asked questions about Community Help.

Adobe Creative Suite 5 Design Premium Help and Support: www.adobe.com/support/creativesuite where you can find and browse Help and Support content on adobe.com.

Adobe TV: http://tv.adobe.com is an online video resource for expert instruction and inspiration about Adobe products, including a How To channel to get you started with your product.

Adobe Design Center: www.adobe.com/designcenter offers thoughtful articles on design and design issues, a gallery showcasing the work of top-notch designers, tutorials, and more.

Adobe Developer Connection: www.adobe.com/devnet is your source for technical articles, code samples, and how-to videos that cover Adobe developer products and technologies.

Resources for educators: www.adobe.com/education includes three free curriculums that use an integrated approach to teaching Adobe software and can be used to prepare for the Adobe Certified Associate exams.

Also check out these useful links:

Adobe Forums: http://forums.adobe.com lets you tap into peer-to-peer discussions, questions, and answers on Adobe products.

Adobe Marketplace & Exchange: www.adobe.com/cfusion/exchange is a central resource for finding tools, services, extensions, code samples, and more to supplement and extend your Adobe products.

Adobe Creative Suite 5 Design Premium CS5 product home page: www.adobe.com/products/creativesuite/design.

Adobe Labs: http://labs.adobe.com gives you access to early builds of cutting-edge technology, as well as forums where you can interact with both the Adobe development teams building that technology and other like-minded members of the community.

Adobe certification

The Adobe training and certification programs are designed to help Adobe customers improve and promote their product-proficiency skills. There are four levels of certification:

*   Adobe Certified Associate (ACA)
*   Adobe Certified Expert (ACE)
*   Adobe Certified Instructor (ACI)
*   Adobe Authorized Training Center (AATC)

The Adobe Certified Associate (ACA) credential certifies that individuals have the entry-level skills to plan, design, build, and maintain effective communications using different forms of digital media.

The Adobe Certified Expert program is a way for expert users to upgrade their credentials. You can use Adobe certification as a catalyst for getting a raise, finding a job, or promoting your expertise.

If you are an ACE-level instructor, the Adobe Certified Instructor program takes your skills to the next level and gives you access to a wide range of Adobe resources.

Adobe Authorized Training Centers offer instructor-led courses and training on Adobe products, employing only Adobe Certified Instructors. A directory of AATCs is available at http://partners.adobe.com.

For information on the Adobe Certified programs, visit www.adobe.com/support/certification/main.html.

ADOBE CREATIVE SUITE 5 DESIGN PREMIUM

Deliver innovative ideas in print, web, and mobile design

Discover powerful new creative tools for expressing your ideas and crafting artwork that stands out. Finish your work faster with numerous enhancements to the tools you use every day. Extend the reach of your designs to new media without writing code. Streamline creative reviews and other essential but time-consuming tasks.

This overview discusses some of the key advantages of the Creative Suite 5 Design Premium:

- Exploring new creative realms

- Expressing your ideas faster

- Extending the reach of your designs without writing code

- Maximizing your design time by streamlining critical nondesign tasks.

This chapter introduces each of the Creative Suite 5 Design Premium components. The lessons in the second part of this book will cover specific aspects of using the applications in much more detail.

As a designer, your job is to create content with impact—content that attracts, informs, inspires, and persuades. Often, this means coming up with solutions that no one has ever seen before—including you. With Design Premium, you can translate even your outrageous ideas into reality, moving smoothly and efficiently across multiple media.

Top features in Adobe Photoshop CS5 Extended

- Intelligent selection technology
- Content-Aware Fill
- HDR Pro and HDR Toning
- State-of-the-art raw-image processing
- Extraordinary painting effects
- Puppet Warp
- Automated lens correction
- Easy 3D extrusions with Adobe Repoussé
- Better media management and Web Gallery integration with Adobe Bridge CS5 and Adobe Mini Bridge
- Enhanced 3D realism and rich materials
- Better 3D performance and workflow
- User-inspired productivity enhancements
- New GPU-accelerated features
- Streamlined creative reviews through integration with Adobe CS Review
- Faster performance with cross-platform 64-bit support

● **Note:** CS Live services are complimentary for a limited time. See www.adobe.com/go/cslive for details.

Explore new creative realms

Exciting new tools in Creative Suite 5 Design Premium software let you imagine daring creative possibilities in the confidence that you can make them real. User-inspired enhancements and simplified workflows help you achieve more efficiency in everyday design and production tasks. Improved integration and more interface consistency between Creative Suite components allow you to draw on your existing expertise to venture into new creative territory: Begin where you're most at home (usually Photoshop, Illustrator, or InDesign) and then switch easily to Flash, Flash Catalyst Dreamweaver, Fireworks, or Acrobat Pro software for refinement, production, and high-quality output for print, web, or mobile.

The Design Premium suite also provides access to CS Live online services that enable you to collaborate from within your design software.

The second part of this book provides a hands-on tour of some of the most compelling new and enhanced features in Design Premium. The lessons focus on various points within two sample projects. One is a complex cross-media creative project based on a fictitious movie called *Double Identity*, and another is a fictitious magazine called *Local* that exists in print and online versions, both originating from Adobe InDesign. You will step through a workflow that allows you to experience the seamless integration across the various components of Design Premium, first working with assets in Photoshop and Illustrator and then laying out in InDesign and creating a SWF file for viewing in Adobe Flash Player. Next you will learn how to take your content to Flash Professional to add interactive content. You will work with a website mock-up in Fireworks, and then take it into Dreamweaver for final production. Finally, you'll see how to test your content for mobile devices using Adobe Device Central CS5 software.

Extraordinary painting effects in Photoshop CS5 Extended

With a new Mixer Brush, a Bristle Tips feature, and a new mechanism for blending colors, Photoshop CS5 redefines the way you paint. You can take advantage of more natural and realistic painting effects, making it easy to take your imagery and designs in new artistic directions.

The Mixer Brush lets you define multiple colors on a single tip, and then mix and blend them with the underlying hues on your canvas, achieving creative results that rival traditional painting media. When starting with a photo original, you can use a dry, empty brush to blend the existing colors while at the same time adding a painterly effect to the image. Mixer Brush settings provide extensive control over the wetness of the canvas colors, the load rate that determines amount of paint loaded on the brush, the mixing rate between brush and canvas colors, and whether the brush is refilled, cleaned, or both after each painting stroke.

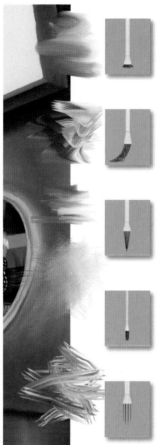

The new Mixer Brush in Photoshop CS5 helps make it easy to take a sketch and turn it into a painting.

The blending abilities of the Mixer Brush, combined with variations in texture provided by Bristle Tips, provide better creative painting control. The Bristle Brush Preview (see insets above) displays a live view of the brush tip as you paint.

In conjunction with these new mixing features, Photoshop CS5 incorporates unprecedented control over stroke characteristics of its painting tools with Bristle Tips. Bristle Qualities define key bristle properties such as shape, length, stiffness, thickness, angle, and spacing, which affect how the color is laid on the image as you paint.

The Bristle Brush Preview feature provides a visual representation of these changes. You can save your tip configurations for future use, allowing you to build a custom collection of Bristle Tips to experiment with when using Photoshop brush tools.

● **Note:** CS Live services are complimentary for a limited time. See www.adobe.com/go/cslive for details.

Fluid vector painting in Adobe Illustrator CS5

In Illustrator CS5, a number of new features have been introduced that make designing with strokes even more powerful and flexible. You can finely control stroke width, dashes, arrowheads, and how brushes stretch along a path. And improvements in corner handling mean that stroke shapes behave predictably in tight angles or around sharp points.

Variable-width strokes. Draw strokes with variable widths that you can quickly and smoothly adjust at any point, symmetrically or along either side. You can create custom width profiles that you can save and subsequently apply to any stroke.

Dashed line control. Control alignment of dashes on a stroke. Now enjoy symmetrical dashes around corners and at the ends of open paths with lengths adjusted automatically to fit. Toggle between adjusted and preserved dashes and gaps.

Precise arrowheads. Work in a completely new way with arrowheads. Pick an arrowhead shape and control placement and scaling from within the Stroke panel. You can even choose whether to lock the tip or base of the arrowhead to the path endpoint.

Stretch control for brushes. Define how art and pattern brushes scale along a path. Choose areas of the brush graphic you want to stretch and those you want to keep in proportion. For example, you may need to elongate the middle of a banner graphic while keeping the detailed, curly ends of the banner from stretching.

Brushes with corner control. Apply art and pattern brushes to a path and get clean results, even at tight bends or corners. Where strokes of different widths join or they form obtuse or acute angles, choose options to properly fill points where joins occur.

Bristle Brush. The new Bristle Brush provides breakthrough painting control—you can paint with vectors that resemble real-world brush strokes. You can set bristle characteristics such as size, length, thickness, and stiffness; set brush shape and bristle density; and set paint opacity, which uses transparency variations to simulate lifelike blending. When you have chosen the perfect characteristics for your Bristle Brush, you can save it for later use.

With the Bristle Brush you can achieve the expressiveness of natural media like watercolors and oils—but with the scalability and editability of vectors. Get the most out of the Bristle Brush using a tablet with a Wacom 6D Art Pen, which responds automatically to pressure, bearing, and tilt, plus provides 360-degree barrel rotation and an accurate brush preview.

The Bristle Brush in Illustrator CS5 can be used in a variety of ways. You can paint traditionally, or you can brush along text shapes to create scrubby or soft-edged type. This text logo works perfectly on the web or on a billboard because it's all purely vector.

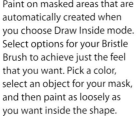

Paint on masked areas that are automatically created when you choose Draw Inside mode. Select options for your Bristle Brush to achieve just the feel that you want. Pick a color, select an object for your mask, and then paint as loosely as you want inside the shape.

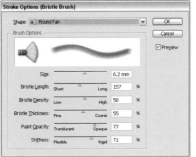

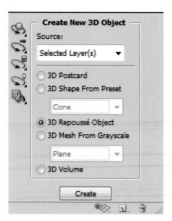

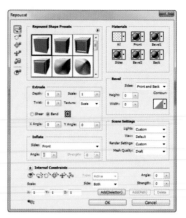

Easily create unique new 3D objects with the settings in the Create New 3D Object section of the 3D panel in Photoshop CS5 Extended.

Use the extrusion settings and controls in the Repoussé dialog box to quickly style your 3D model.

Once your extrusion is created, you can adjust a variety of its characteristics. In this example, the Scale (left), Inflate And Bevel (middle), and Bend And Depth (right) settings have been altered to change the design.

Easy 3D extrusions with Adobe Repoussé (Photoshop CS5 Extended only)

Repoussé is an ancient metalworking technique for embossing artwork on the surface of metals such as gold, silver, copper, tin, and bronze. Inspired by this traditional technique, Photoshop Extended offers a powerful new feature for creating eye-catching 3D artwork.

Use Adobe Repoussé to easily convert 2D artwork into 3D objects and then create depth by altering the extrusion properties of the 3D model. Easily extrude text to create logos and 3D artwork for use in websites, video frames, or layouts.

Starting with a text layer, a path, a selection, or a layer mask, you can convert the content to 3D with the Create New 3D Object section of the 3D panel. After the conversion is complete, you can alter the look of your 3D model by manipulating its key extrusion properties—Depth, Scale, Bend, Shear, Inflate, or Twist—in the Repoussé dialog box.

In addition to manipulating these properties, you can inflate the front or back of the extrusion and/or apply a custom bevel. Sections of objects (internal subpaths) can also be inflated by creating a selection first and then adjusting the Internal Constraints settings in the Repoussé dialog box. The 3D Axis widget allows on canvas rotation of the model.

Changing the look of your Repoussé 3D models in Photoshop CS5 Extended can be achieved in just a few clicks, thanks to a vast library of materials to select from and an improved method of applying them. Left: Repoussé model without materials. Right: Model with materials applied.

Express your ideas faster

CS5 Design Premium includes dozens of features designed to reduce the number of steps required to complete common tasks. Photoshop, Illustrator, InDesign, and Dreamweaver—the tools you use every day—all offer numerous enhancements to help you make fast work of your next project.

Truer Edge selection technology in Photoshop CS5 Extended

Photoshop CS5 takes the time and frustration out of making precise image selections and masks, providing you a faster way to extract subjects from their backgrounds and create realistic composites. New intelligent selection technology offers better edge detection and faster, more accurate masking results of complex subjects, like hair. Automatic color decontamination helps you eliminate background color around the edges of a selection, resulting in more seamless compositions when placing extracted subjects on new backgrounds.

Experienced Photoshop users know that the best selections are created by constantly adapting the selection technique for differences in the subject's edges—one method for hair and another for the edge of a building. With Photoshop CS5, you can produce highly accurate masks and selections faster and more simply than before with a set of new adaptive selection-edge modification controls. Smart Radius automatically matches the best selection approach with the subject's changing edge characteristics, and the extra view modes assist you in previewing the quality of your selections. The Refine Radius and Erase Refinements tools customize your masks and selections as you make them. These tools, in combination with the color decontamination settings, help eliminate any residual background color from around the edges of your selections.

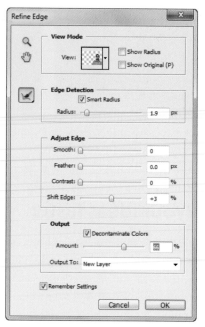

Edge Detection in Photoshop CS5 uses adaptive selection technology to create selections of different edge types, such as along a simple solid line like this man's jacket, or a more complex selection, such as his hair.

The ability to create accurate selections is made easier with the Edge Detection controls in the updated Refine Edge dialog box.

The Edge Detection and Decontaminate Colors features help you make highly precise selections of complex subjects quickly and easily, enabling faster, more accurate compositing of multiple images. Top Right: Original. Left: After refining the selection edge in Photoshop CS5. Bottom Right: Extracted subject combined with new background.

Simplified object selection and editing in Adobe InDesign CS5

Perform repetitive layout tasks efficiently in InDesign CS5. Numerous improvements can help make tasks such as aligning and distributing objects or customizing frame corners faster and easier.

Multiple transformations with a single tool. You can use one tool to select, align, distribute, rotate, resize, reposition, crop, and scale frames and frame content. InDesign CS5 dynamically switches to the right tool for the job, so you never need to lift your mouse from the layout. The new Content Grabber lets you quickly reposition content within a frame, just by clicking and dragging. A real-time crop preview helps you position the content precisely where you want it.

Gap tool. Adjust the white space between objects to dynamically reposition page items while maintaining design relationships. Shift the white space up or down, left or right, without having to crop or resize each object on the page. You can even expand or contract the white space, dynamically resizing or cropping adjacent objects accordingly. The new Auto-Fit feature keeps the relationship between the object and its frame consistent as you resize the frame.

When Auto-Fit is enabled, InDesign CS5 honors object fitting settings (such as Center in Frame) to maintain the relationship between objects and their frames as you adjust the gap between objects. Simply drag the Gap tool to adjust the cropping of all the abutting images. Control/Command-drag the Gap tool to resize a gap instead of moving it.

Live Corner Effects. Drag the corners of a frame to dynamically change the radius and shape of the frame directly in the layout. Modify one corner at a time or all four simultaneously.

Top features in InDesign CS5

- Interactive documents and presentations
- Simplified object selection and editing
- Integration with Adobe CS Review
- Multiple page sizes
- Track text changes
- Paragraphs that span and split columns
- All-new Layers panel
- Production enhancements
- Print to digital
- Live captions

● **Note:** CS Live services are complimentary for a limited time. See www.adobe.com/go/cslive for details.

Click to make the corners active, and then drag the corner diamonds to new positions. On-object controls make it simple to dynamically change the look and feel of a frame as you design.

Easy grid placement. Take the tedium out of placing images in a grid, as in a directory or catalog. Simply press arrow keys to add columns and rows for images or threaded text frames.

Multiple page sizes in a single InDesign CS5 document

Simplify file management by creating pages of different sizes in a single document. Whether you're designing marketing collateral, brand identity deliverables, or a magazine layout with complex folds, keeping all of a project's assets in the same file shortens design and production time.

The new Page Selection tool makes it easy to select individual pages, which you can resize using options in the Control panel. You can easily share design assets by applying the same master pages to pages of varying sizes. With the Page Selection tool, you can even reposition the master page content for different layouts: Select the page, select Show Master Page Overlay in the Control panel, and then drag the edge of the master page to position it over the page.

The ability to combine multiple page sizes in InDesign CS5 simplifies the layout of documents with complex folds, such as this magazine with a cover flap. Not only can you create pages with different sizes in a document—you can include them in a single spread.

More efficient CSS-based designs with Dreamweaver CS5

If you're an aspiring or novice web designer who prefers designing pages to writing code, you'll appreciate CSS Inspect. CSS Inspect lets you lay out web pages based on Cascading Style Sheets (CSS) more easily—without diving into code or using additional software. For designers who are new to web design or who want to deepen their knowledge of CSS, CSS Inspect makes it much easier to learn about and work with CSS-based web pages.

In the past, troubleshooting CSS-based page elements was not an intuitive process. First, you previewed the web page in a browser and used a browser plug-in or utility to search for the page element you wanted to modify. Then you viewed the element's CSS rules and properties, noted the desired changes, and switched back to Dreamweaver to implement them.

Now you can accomplish this task seamlessly within Dreamweaver. CSS Inspect displays the CSS box model properties—including padding, border, and margin—so you can quickly locate and modify a CSS-based element. Simply select the element in Live View to view its corresponding CSS rules and properties in the CSS Styles panel. Make your edits directly in the panel or in the Code window and see the changes reflected immediately.

Top features in Dreamweaver CS5

- Support for PHP-based content management systems
- Dynamically Related Files
- Live View navigation
- Enhanced CSS tools
- Integration with Adobe BrowserLab
- Enhanced support for Subversion
- PHP custom class code hinting
- Site-specific code hints
- Enhanced CSS starter layouts
- Simple site setup
- Integration with Business Catalyst

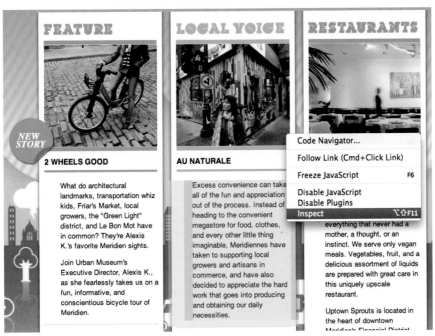

Dreamweaver CS5 highlights box model properties with colors so you can visually inspect individual page elements.

Quickly and easily disable and reenable CSS properties directly from the CSS Styles panel in Dreamweaver CS5. Disabling a CSS property simply comments out the specified property without actually deleting it, and the affected property is no longer rendered. This convenient option for toggling CSS properties on and off, coupled with the ability to inspect CSS, allows you to remain in your editing environment throughout the development process, eliminating the time-consuming process of previewing in the browser and troubleshooting with browser-based tools.

Dreamweaver CS5 gives you the freedom to experiment with and troubleshoot CSS by toggling individual CSS properties on and off as you view the box model changes in color.

Extend the reach of your designs without writing code

When designers collaborate with developers to produce interactive content, they sometimes have to compromise their creative vision. With CS5 Design Premium, designers can work on interactive content and media-rich projects themselves using familiar tools, skills, and design processes—and without touching a line of code. Here are just two ways you can design and deliver your work in digital media using skills you already have:

- Craft interactive content that adds depth and impact to web pages, create artwork in Photoshop or Illustrator, and then use new Flash Catalyst to define interactions for elements such as buttons, sliders, and scroll bars. When you're finished, export the interactive content as a SWF file. With Flash Catalyst, you can also design user interface elements for websites or applications and even create Adobe AIR applications that run from the desktop.

- Optimize a print layout for onscreen delivery, simply open the layout in InDesign and use new panels to add interactivity, animation, video, and/or sound.

Now you can take your designs in exciting new directions and maintain design control without becoming a programmer.

Interactive content with Flash Catalyst CS5

New from Adobe and built specifically for designers, Flash Catalyst enables you to create interactive content without writing code. With Flash Catalyst, you can take advantage of the expressiveness of Flash technology and the ubiquity of Flash Player to deliver compelling interactivity, video, and audio to computers around the world.

Transform artwork created in Photoshop, Illustrator, or Fireworks into high-quality interactive content that can liven up your web pages or make complex information engaging and easier to understand. Design simple projects, such as an interactive portfolio site or product brochure, that you can complete yourself in SWF format. Or tackle more complex projects such as a user interface for a web application built in collaboration with a developer. While you design visually in the foreground, Flash Catalyst generates Adobe Flex code in the background.

Begin by importing a design comp created in Photoshop, Illustrator, or Fireworks into your Flash Catalyst project. Use easy-to-understand menu commands to convert individual elements into functional interactive components such as buttons, sliders, and scroll bars. When you're finished polishing your interactive content, you can add it to web pages, embed it in a PDF file, or run it as a self-contained Adobe AIR application directly on the desktop.

In Flash Catalyst, simply select objects created in Photoshop, Illustrator, or Fireworks and indicate the interactive function you want it to have. For example, draw scroll bar parts in Illustrator and use menus in Flash Catalyst to assign scroll bar functions to the parts.

Dynamic digital documents in InDesign CS5

Engage and inform readers and clients with documents and presentations that integrate interactivity, animation, sound, and video. Help reduce costs by creating interactivity directly in InDesign.

New intuitive panels help you add rich media to page layouts:

Animation panel. Apply the same motion presets included in Flash Professional CS5, or add your own custom presets to InDesign to instantly animate objects on the page without writing code. Options in the Animation panel let you specify duration, speed, rotation, scale, and opacity. Quickly edit a motion path using the Pen tool, and convert any path—even one you import from Illustrator—into a custom motion path with the click of a button.

Object States panel. Create multi-state objects that indicate which button is selected, display images in a slide show, or show versions of text in different languages. Multi-state objects are page items that have multiple appearances. Object states can be images, text frames, or any other objects or groups you want to display when someone clicks or rolls over an interactive button while viewing an interactive document. For example, you might create a multi-state object that consists of multiple images to create a click-through slide show; when the viewer clicks a button, the next image appears.

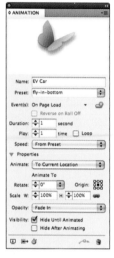

You can preview motion presets in the Animation panel in InDesign CS5. The butterfly proxy demonstrates the effect. Use the Pen tool to edit any motion path—even one created by a motion preset.

In InDesign CS5, manage states in the Object States panel. You can rearrange states to change the order in which they appear.

Timing panel. Control animation timing and playback without having to use a timeline to add keyframes or create motion tweens. Use the Timing panel to determine when objects such as bullet points in a presentation or images on a page should animate in the interactive document. For example, animations can be triggered to play when the page loads, when the page is clicked, or when a button is clicked. Loop the animation or play it a specific number of times. Link objects to animate simultaneously with the same or different durations.

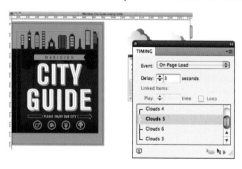

The Timing panel in InDesign CS5 provides an intuitive way to control when animations begin to play and how many times they repeat.

Media panel. Preview and scrub through placed video files without leaving InDesign. You can select a frame from the video sequence to represent the video in your InDesign document before the video plays, and even create navigation points that determine which parts of the video play when you click a button or otherwise trigger an action.

Entice viewers to watch an embedded video by selecting a frame to represent it on an InDesign CS5 layout.

Preview panel. Take animations, buttons, and other interactive elements for a test drive without leaving InDesign. You no longer have to reexport your content every time you edit rich media elements—interactivity, animation, video, or sound—just to see how the change affects the document. Instead, preview and test a selection, the page, or the entire document before you export your final SWF file.

Superior text layout and typography in Flash Professional CS5

Designers have come to expect rich typographic control in applications like InDesign and Illustrator. However, it's been extremely difficult or even impossible to set professional-level typography on the web—until now. With the Text Layout Framework support in Flash Professional CS5, designers can take advantage of rich typographical controls, including:

- Advanced text styling such as kerning, ligatures, tracking, leading, superscript, subscript, discretionary hyphens, margins, hypertext, baseline shift, typographic case, digit case (oldstyle/lining figures), and digit width (proportional/tabular figures).

- Advanced text-layout controls including threaded text blocks; the selection, editing, and flowing of text across multiple columns; linked images; text wrap; and inline images (supporting PNG, JPEG, SWF, or any Flash Player DisplayObject). Tab stops and CSS anti-aliasing are also supported.

Top features in Flash Professional CS5

- New text engine
- Ability to distribute content virtually anywhere
- XML-based FLA source files
- Code Snippets panel
- Enhanced ActionScript editor
- Improved Creative Suite integration
- Flash Builder integration
- Spring for Bones
- Video improvements
- New Deco drawing tools

With the new text engine in Flash Professional CS5, you can take advantage of rich typographical controls, including threaded and multi-column text.

Simplified mobile content design in Fireworks CS5 and Device Central CS5

Easily experiment with designing for mobile devices. Integration between Fireworks and Device Central makes it easy to set up a Fireworks project and preview it in Device Central. In Device Central, choose File > New Document In Fireworks, select a target device, and then click Create. Fireworks then creates a new project with the correct pixel dimensions of the target device's display. Use the visual prototyping tools in Fireworks to craft your mobile content, and then choose File > Preview In Device Central to emulate your content using the updated online library of device profiles. When you've perfected your prototype, hand it off for development in Flash Professional or Dreamweaver.

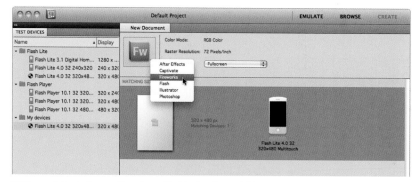

With a mobile device profile selected in Device Central CS5, you can use the New Document panel to create a new Fireworks document that's already set up with document settings that match the selected device.

Maximize your design time by streamlining critical nondesign tasks

CS5 Design Premium integrates with Adobe CS Live online services to help you bring efficiencies to design and production activities.

Accelerate reviews through integration with Adobe CS Review

Enjoy faster, more efficient creative reviews with CS Review, a new Adobe CS Live online service that integrates with components of CS5 Design Premium. Initiate shared reviews with just a few clicks from within Photoshop, Illustrator, or InDesign—simply click Access CS Live in the Application bar to open the CS Review panel. Then create a new review, add your layout or artwork, and invite colleagues or clients to view it online. They receive an email invitation with a link—one click and they see the document displayed in their web browser.

Note: CS Live services are complimentary for a limited time. See www.adobe.com/go/cslive for details.

With commenting tools so easy to use there's practically no learning curve, your reviewers can give overall feedback or comment on a specific region or text selection. Their comments appear in the CS Review panel, and everyone can view and reply to each other's comments. Clicking a comment takes you to the specific element the comment refers to, so you can easily match each comment to the right element in your layout or artwork.

With simple sharing, easy access to reviews, and centralized comments, CS Review can help speed up the review process so you can finish your project on time and within budget.

Reviewers add comments within the browser online. Those comments appear in the CS Review panel in InDesign CS5. Thumbnails give you context for the feedback, making it easier to find and address comments.

Note: CS Live services are complimentary for a limited time. See www.adobe.com/go/cslive for details.

Web page preview with Adobe BrowserLab, a CS Live online service

If you've done even a little web design, you know how challenging it can be to predict how a web page will appear in different browsers and operating systems. Until now, the best way to preview web content required buying costly hardware, installing multiple browsers, and maintaining testing labs. In addition, opening and comparing pages in multiple browsers on multiple machines is tedious and time-consuming.

Adobe BrowserLab allows you to compare your web pages and applications in multiple browsers without having the specific operating system or browser installed on your local computer.

Another new CS Live online service, Adobe BrowserLab, is an easier, faster solution for previewing web pages on leading browsers and operating systems—on demand. Whether you're creating web pages yourself or previewing pages that you've designed and handed off to a developer for production, BrowserLab enables you to ensure that your work will appear as you intend.

BrowserLab works by taking screen shots of your web pages in different browsers, and then displaying them in the BrowserLab application window. You can preview a page in a single browser or compare the page in two browsers side by side. You can also compare screen shots in onionskin view—with one image superimposed over another—and control the relative transparency of the two images. Built-in rules and guides enable you to make pixel-perfect comparisons between images. Use the service from your web browser to test pages that you've posted to a server, or take advantage of integration between BrowserLab and Dreamweaver to test your pages directly from within Dreamweaver without publishing them to a server. Simply open a page in Dreamweaver, choose File > Preview In Browser > Adobe Browser Lab, sign in, and choose the browsers in which you want to preview the page. Create and configure sets of browsers you want to test. And because BrowserLab is an online service, you can get your results in real time, from virtually any computer connected to the web.

Accelerate your workflow with Adobe CS Live

Adobe CS Live is a set of online services that harness the connectivity of the web and integrate with Adobe Creative Suite 5 to simplify the creative review process, speed up website compatibility testing, deliver important web user intelligence, and more, allowing you to focus on creating your most impactful work. CS Live services are complimentary for a limited time* and can be accessed online or from within Creative Suite 5 applications.

Adobe BrowserLab is for web designers and developers who need to preview and test their web pages on multiple browsers and operating systems. Unlike other browser-compatibility solutions, BrowserLab renders screenshots virtually on demand with multiple viewing and diagnostic tools, and can be used with Dreamweaver CS5 to preview local content and different states of interactive pages. Being an online service, BrowserLab has fast development cycles, with greater flexibility for expanded browser support and updated functionality.

Adobe CS Review is for creative professionals who want a new level of efficiency in the creative review process. Unlike other services that offer online review of creative content, only CS Review lets you publish a review to the web directly from within InDesign, Photoshop, Photoshop Extended, and Illustrator and view reviewer comments back in the originating Creative Suite application.

Acrobat.com is for creative professionals who need to work with a cast of colleagues and clients in order to get a creative project from creative brief to final product. Acrobat.com is a set of online services that includes web conferencing, online file-sharing, and workspaces. Unlike collaborating via e-mail and attending time-consuming in-person meetings, Acrobat.com brings people to your work instead of sending files to people, so you can get the business side of the creative process done faster, together, from any location.

Adobe Story is for creative professionals, producers, and writers working on or with scripts. Story is a collaborative script-development tool that turns scripts into metadata that can be used with the Adobe CS5 Production Premium tools to streamline workflows and create video assets.

SiteCatalyst NetAverages is for web and mobile professionals who want to optimize their projects for wider audiences. NetAverages provides intelligence on how users are accessing the web, which helps reduce guesswork early in the creative process. You can access aggregate user data such as browser type, operating system, mobile device profile, screen resolution, and more, which can be shown over time. The data is derived from visitor activity to participating Omniture SiteCatalyst customer sites. Unlike other web intelligence solutions, NetAverages innovatively displays data using Flash, creating an engaging experience that is robust yet easy to follow.

You can access CS Live three different ways:

1   Set up access when you register your Creative Suite 5 products, and get complimentary access that includes all of the features and workflow benefits of using CS Live with CS5.

2   Set up access by signing up online, and get complimentary access to CS Live services for a limited time. Note that this option does not give you access to the services from within your products.

3   Desktop product trials include a 30-day trial of CS Live services.

CS Live services are complimentary for a limited time. See www.adobe.com/go/cslive for details.

Adobe BrowserLab is a fast, flexible, and convenient way to make sure your web designs look exactly the way you intend them to look, no matter what browser, computer, and operating system is used to view them.

The Adobe Creative Suite 5 Family

Discover breakthrough interactive design tools that enable you to create, deliver, and optimize beautiful, high-impact digital experiences across media and devices. Create once and deliver that same experience virtually everywhere, thanks to the highly anticipated releases of the Adobe Flash Player 10.1 and Adobe AIR 2 runtimes. Maximize the impact of what you've created through integration of signature Omniture technologies. You can choose from several editions of Adobe Creative Suite 5 to meet your specific needs.

Adobe Creative Suite 5 Design Premium

Adobe Creative Suite 5 Design Premium software is the ultimate toolkit for designers who need to express their wildest ideas with precision; work fluidly across media; and produce exceptional results in print, web, interactive, and mobile design. Craft eye-catching images and graphics, lay out stunning pages, build standards-based websites, create interactive content without writing code, and extend page layouts for viewing with eBook reading devices.

Adobe Creative Suite 5 Design Premium software offers a host of productivity features for print design, including more precise image selection in Adobe Photoshop, enhanced object editing in Adobe InDesign, and perspective drawing in Adobe Illustrator. Revolutionize everyday creative work with innovative painting tools in Photoshop and Illustrator.

Design Premium combines full new versions of InDesign CS5, Illustrator CS5, Photoshop CS5 Extended, Flash Professional CS5, Flash Catalyst CS5, Dreamweater CS5, Fireworks CS5, and Acrobat 9 Pro, and with Adobe Bridge CS5 and Adobe Device Central CS5.

Adobe Creative Suite 5 Design Standard

For design and production professionals focused on print publishing who do not need the full-fledged web, interactive, and mobile design capabilities of Dreamweaver, Flash, and Fireworks, or the advanced video, animation, and 3D editing tools in Photoshop Extended, Adobe offers Adobe Creative Suite 5 Design Standard software.

Adobe Creative Suite 5 Web Premium

Adobe Creative Suite 5 Web Premium software makes it easier to create standards-based websites and immersive digital experiences. With Adobe Dreamweaver CS5 and integrated tools in the Adobe Flash Platform, you can design and develop content for delivery virtually anywhere.

Use a comprehensive toolkit that includes Flash Catalyst CS5 to design interactive content without writing code, Flash Professional CS5 to create rich free-form expressive content, and Flash Builder 4 Standard to develop rich Internet applications.

Build standards-based websites with Dreamweaver CS5, the industry-leading web authoring tool. Develop with PHP and content management frameworks like WordPress, Joomla!, or Drupal, and design productively with CSS inspection tools.

Get fast and accurate browser compatibility testing, and accelerate tasks such as collaborative content creation and reviews of presentations and project pitches with new CS Live online services.

Note: CS Live services are complimentary for a limited time. See www.adobe.com/go/cslive for details.

Web Premium combines full new versions of Dreamweaver CS5, Flash Catalyst CS5, Flash Professional CS5, Flash Builder CS5, Photoshop CS5 Extended, Illustrator CS5, Acrobat 9 Pro, Fireworks CS5, and Contribute CS5, and with Adobe Bridge CS5 and Adobe Device Central CS5.

Adobe Creative Suite 5 Production Premium

Conquer today's deadlines and tomorrow's challenges with Adobe Creative Suite 5 Production Premium software, the ultimate video production toolkit. Craft video productions, motion graphics, visual effects, and interactive experiences with high-performance, industry-leading creative tools. Boost your productivity with tightly integrated components that deliver breakthrough performance and smooth production workflows, giving you the power to produce engaging media for virtually any screen.

With the latest versions of Adobe's best-of-breed video, audio, and design tools, CS5 Production Premium offers enhancements that help you work more efficiently when tackling a broad spectrum of planning, production, and postproduction tasks. Each component offers a familiar user interface and integrates with other components for a complete, end-to-end toolset that accelerates video editing workflows from scriptwriting through postproduction.

For motion graphic designers and visual effects artists, CS5 Production Premium offers best-of-breed video, animation, compositing, audio, and design tools that feel like a natural extension of your creative process. Work more efficiently with high-resolution projects and benefit from tight integration between Adobe Photoshop Extended, Illustrator, and Adobe Premiere Pro.

Production Premium combines full new versions of Premiere Pro CS5, After Effects CS5, Photoshop CS5 Extended, Illustrator CS5, Flash Catalyst CS5, Flash Professional CS5, Soundbooth CS5, Adobe On Location CS5, and Encore CS5, and with Adobe Bridge CS5, Adobe Device Central CS5, and Dynamic Link.

Adobe Creative Suite 5 Master Collection

Tell your story from start to finish with one comprehensive offering. Adobe Creative Suite 5 Master Collection software enables you to design and develop amazing work, collaborate effectively, and deliver virtually anywhere.

Craft a corporate identity using Illustrator CS5 to engage your audience online, extending your creative reach. Use new Flash Catalyst CS5 to make your project part of an expressive, interactive interface without writing code.

Design and deliver immersive experiences. Use Flash Professional CS5 to engage your audience with microsites and casual games that present your designs consistently across desktops, browsers, and mobile devices.

Take your story to any screen. Enhance HD video productions with high-resolution imagery from Photoshop CS5 Extended. Add intricate effects using After Effects CS5, and edit dramatically faster in Adobe Premiere Pro CS5.

Production Premium combines full new versions of Photoshop CS5 Extended, Illustrator CS5, InDesign CS5, Acrobat 9 Pro, Flash Catalyst CS5, Flash Professional CS5, Flash Builder 4, Dreamweaver CS5, Fireworks CS5, Contribute CS5, Premiere Pro CS5, After Effects CS5, Soundbooth CS5, Adobe On Location CS5, and Encore CS5, and with Adobe Bridge CS5, Adobe Device Central CS5, and Dynamic Link.

Common Features

No matter which edition of Creative Suite 5 you choose, you gain a toolset with integration that's enhanced by the following:

Adobe Bridge CS5 software is a powerful media manager that provides centralized access to all your creative assets.

Adobe Device Central CS5 software simplifies the production of innovative and compelling content for mobile phones and consumer electronics devices. Adobe Device Central CS5 now offers support for HTML and the latest versions of Adobe Flash Player software.

● **Note:** CS Live services are complimentary for a limited time. See www.adobe.com/go/cslive for details.

Bring creative reviews directly into your design workflow thanks to Adobe CS Review, a new Adobe CS Live online service that integrates with your design software. CS Live services are complimentary for a limited time.

In Production Premium CS5 and Master Collection, Adobe Dynamic Link gives you tighter-than-ever integration when moving assets between Adobe After Effects CS5, Adobe Premiere Pro CS5, and Encore CS5. An integral part of Adobe Creative Suite 5 Production Premium and Master Collection software, Dynamic Link enables you to work faster and stay in the creative flow by eliminating intermediate rendering when you make changes to assets—whether you're editing a sequence of clips in Adobe Premiere Pro, changing a composition in After Effects, or refining a project in Encore.

1 SETTING UP BASIC ASSETS

Lesson Overview

The way you set up your documents and create your assets will affect how easily and efficiently you can design your work. This lesson will introduce you to some important skills and concepts:

- Organizing your work in Adobe Bridge
- Drawing expressively with the Bristle Brush in Illustrator
- Refining a vector graphic in Illustrator with the Blob Brush tool
- Setting up multiple Illustrator artboards for design variations
- Drawing in perspective in Illustrator
- Removing a background in Photoshop Extended
- Removing unwanted objects in Photoshop Extended
- Creating a 3D object in Photoshop Extended

 You'll probably need between one and two hours to complete this lesson.

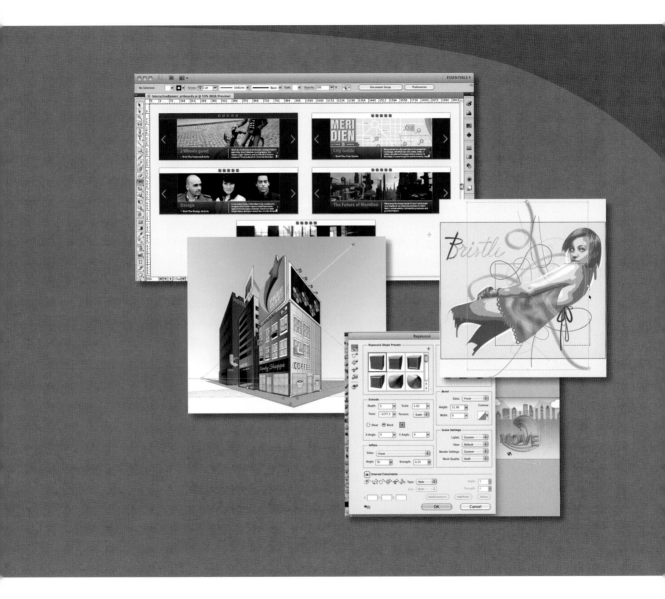

In this lesson, you'll be working on exciting projects: painting with a pattern to add pizzazz to a graphic, creating design variations on their own artboards, and manipulating a 3D comp. You'll be preparing assets that you'll use in a printed and interactive brochure and Flash animation in lessons later in this book.

Note: Before you start working on this lesson, make sure that you've installed the Creative Suite 5 Design Premium software on your computer, and that you have correctly copied the Lessons folder from the CD in the back of this book onto your computer's hard disk (see "Copying the Classroom in a Book files" on page 2).

Organizing your work with Bridge

In this lesson, you'll set up some of the basic assets that you'll use for the projects in this book. Two projects are the basis for the lessons in this book: Promotional materials for an imaginary film noir called *Double Identity*, and a fictional regional magazine called *Local* which has both print and interactive online components. You'll be working in Adobe Bridge, Adobe Illustrator, Adobe Photoshop Extended, and Adobe Acrobat.

Adobe Bridge CS5 provides integrated, centralized access to your project files and enables you to quickly browse through your creative assets visually—regardless of what format they're in—making it easy for you to locate, organize, and view your files.

Adding folders to your Favorites

To help you access your files easily, Adobe Bridge adds your Pictures and Documents folders to the Favorites panel by default. You can add as many of your frequently used applications, folders, and documents as you like. In Bridge Preferences you can even specify which of the default favorites you want to keep in the Favorites panel.

After you've copied the Lessons folder from the *Adobe Creative Suite 5 Classroom in a Book* disc to your hard disk, it's a good idea to add your Lessons folder to the Favorites panel in Bridge, so that the files you'll use for the lessons in this book will be only one click away. You could add your Lesson01 folder right below that and keep it there while you work through this chapter.

1 Start Adobe Bridge CS5. At the top of the Bridge window, make sure the Essentials workspace is selected.

2 Navigate to your Lessons folder, and then select the Lesson01 folder in the Content panel. Drag it into the Favorites panel in the left panel group and drop it under the Pictures folder.

Tip: You can also quickly add a folder to your Favorites by right-clicking/Control-clicking the folder in the Content panel and choosing Add To Favorites from the context menu.

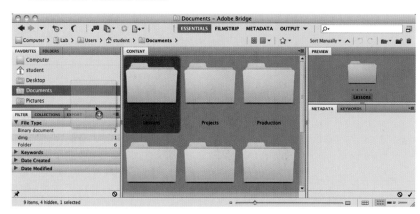

Now your Lessons files are easily accessible. While working through the lessons in this book you'll save so much time that it'll be unimaginable to work any other way!

Adding metadata

All your documents contain some metadata, such as information about the device with which they were created. You can use Bridge to add your own metadata to a single file or to multiple files at the same time—without having to open the application specific to those files.

In this first exercise you'll see how easy it is to add metadata to a file and learn some different ways to mark it, which will make it easier to find and sort.

1 In Bridge, navigate to your Lesson01 folder to see the files inside. You'll be working with these files later in this lesson.

2 Select the file Red_car_3D.psd and note the Metadata panel in the right panel group.

3 In the Metadata panel, expand the IPTC Core panel, and type **red, oldtimer** in the Keywords text field.

▶ **Tip:** If you can't read all your filenames or the thumbnail images are not big enough, you can enlarge them by using the Zoom slider at the lower-right corner.

What you just did is enter two keywords, using a comma to separate them so that they are entered individually. You can also enter keywords using the Keywords panel that you may see grouped with the Metadata panel, but when you're entering many types of metadata you may find it more convenient to enter them in the Metadata panel along with everything else.

4 Press Enter/Return to apply your entries.

When you search for this file in the future, the metadata you just added will help you to find this specific file. Bridge looks in the metadata fields when you search for a file in Bridge, and in addition, the search features built into Microsoft Windows and Mac OS X also look for keywords to improve their search results.

● **Note:** If you forget to press Enter/Return after typing keywords, a confirmation dialog will appear when you click outside the Metadata panel; click Apply to confirm your entries.

Marking your files with ratings and color labels

When you're working with a large number of files and folders, assigning ratings and labels is a good way to mark a large number of files quickly, making it easier to sort and find them later.

● **Note:** If you don't see rating stars under a thumbnail, enlarge the thumbnail size by dragging to the right the slider at the bottom of the Bridge window, and make sure the View > Show Thumbnail Only command is deselected.

1   In the Content menu, note the five dots above the filename Red_car_3D.psd, indicating that this file has not yet been rated. Click on the third dot, which will apply a three-star rating—it's that easy to rate a file.

You can also mark a file visually by assigning a color label.

2   Choose Label > Approved. Your file is marked with a green color label, which you can also see in the right panel group.

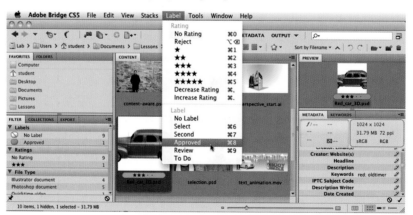

This color labeling system is not only useful to help you quickly spot the images you're looking for, but is also an effective way to sort your images by category, production status, or any other meanings you assign to the labels. This can be a useful organizational tool—especially when different people are working on the same project. You can use the Filter panel to quickly locate files with specific ratings or labels.

About Live Trace

A lot of great design ideas start out as a great pencil sketch on paper. To keep the precious spontaneity of such hand-drawn scribbles, it's best to bring the graphics straight into Illustrator and trace them. Placing a scanned file into Illustrator and automatically tracing the artwork with the Live Trace command is the easiest way to do so. The illustrations below show studies for a logo.

Live Trace automatically turns placed images into detailed vector graphics that are easy to edit, resize, and manipulate without distortion. And, as Illustrator fans know already, Live Trace enables you to produce stunning looking illustrations by changing rasterized images into vector-based drawings. You'll appreciate how quickly you can re-create a scanned drawing onscreen, maintaining its quality and authentic feel.

3 Right-click/Control-click the image of the car again, and this time choose Sort > By Label from the context menu. If you had multiple files with the same label, they would now be grouped in the Content panel. You can change the sort order by toggling View > Sort > Ascending Order.

Synchronizing color management

Using Bridge as your central hub enables you to synchronize the color management settings across all your Creative Suite applications. It's highly recommended to use this feature so that the colors in your images will look the same regardless of which Creative Suite component application you're working with.

There are a range of options for synchronizing color management. You can specify your own color settings in the Color Settings dialog box in the relevant Adobe application, and then apply it to all the other Adobe Creative Suite applications in Bridge, or you can choose one of the Bridge presets.

1 In Bridge, choose Edit > Creative Suite Color Settings.

2   The Suite Color Settings dialog box appears. A message at the top of the dialog
box tells you whether or not the settings are already synchronized. If they are
not, choose North America General Purpose 2 from the color settings menu,
and then click Apply. If the Apply button isn't active, select any setting, then
select North America General Purpose 2 and click Apply.

The message at the top of the Suite Color Settings dialog box should now indicate
that all your CS5 applications use the same color management settings.

Creating artwork in Illustrator

When you're designing graphics such as logos and corporate identities, it's an
absolute must that your design be scalable, because the graphic will be used in a
wide range of applications, from web pages at screen resolution to high-resolution
printed matter or even monumental signage. For designing graphics that need to
be resolution independent, Adobe Illustrator is the world's leading vector-based
application. Today, other applications in the Creative Suite such as InDesign and
Photoshop also let you create vector graphics using the Pen tool (amongst others);
however, your best choice is still Illustrator, because it includes the most comprehensive set of drawing tools.

Bitmap versus vector graphics

Pixel- or raster-based applications such as Photoshop are unbeatable when it comes to producing photographic or continuous-tone images. However, these images are composed of a fixed number of pixels, resulting in a jagged—or pixelated—look when they are enlarged. The illustration below clearly shows the difference between a resolution-independent vector graphic (left) and a pixel-based graphic (right).

With Illustrator, you create vector graphics—artwork that is made up of points, lines, and curves that are expressed as mathematical vectors. Vector-based graphics are resolution independent—they can be scaled to any size without losing quality or crispness.

Creating a vector graphic with the Bristle Brush

You don't need to use a painting program to create expressive brush strokes. In Illustrator CS5, the Bristle Brush gives you the creative possibilities of traditional media like watercolors, oils, and pastels, while also providing the speed, editability, and scalability you expect with vector graphics. If you have a Wacom tablet, you can control Bristle Brush strokes with stylus pressure, and with Wacom Intous tablets you can also control strokes using tilt angle, bearing, and barrel rotation.

1   In your Lesson01 folder, double-click the file bristle_brush.ai.

2   In the Layers panel, make the Model layer visible by clicking to show the eye icon for that layer.

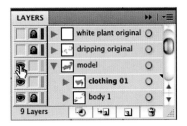

3   With the Selection tool, select the pink dress.

4   In the Tools panel, click the Drawing Modes icon and choose Draw Inside. This will let you draw freely and keep your artwork inside the dress.

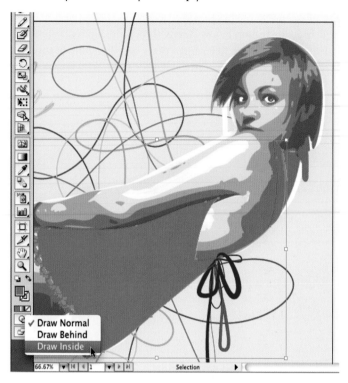

5   Choose Select > Deselect, and then select the Brush tool.

6   Choose Window > Brushes, and then choose New Brush from the Brushes panel menu. In the New Brush dialog box, select Bristle Brush and click OK.

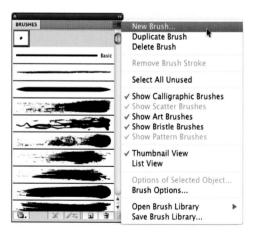

7 In the Bristle Brush Options dialog box, choose Round Fan from the Shape menu. Change the Size to 10mm; you don't need to change anything else. Click OK to close the dialog box.

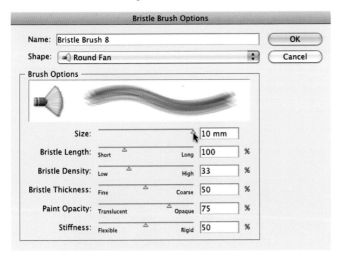

8 In the Tools panel, make sure Stroke color is active, and then in the Swatches panel, select a color that's different than the dress.

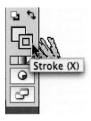

9 Drag the brush inside the dress to paint with broad strokes. Try different colors.

10 With the Selection tool, select the tallest pink swirl behind the model.

11 In the Brushes panel, select the 4.80mm round fan brush. Notice how the swirl now appears as if it had been painted freehand. In this way, you can easily apply Bristle Brush strokes to a path you've already drawn.

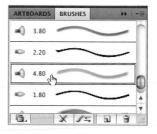

12 Choose File > Save As, navigate to your Lesson01 folder, name the file bristle_brush_done.ai, and click Save. Then close the document.

Refining a vector graphic with the Blob Brush tool

If you have been working with the brushes in Flash and Photoshop, you'll find similarities in the Blob Brush in Illustrator, which enables you to generate a clean vector shape as you paint. Used in combination with the Eraser tool, the Blob Brush provides a truly painterly, intuitive way to create vector shapes—merging your brush strokes into a single, fluid outline that can then be filled with solid color or painted with a gradient or even a pattern.

In this exercise you'll design a variation on an existing graphic by refining the outline of a masthead logo that was traced from handwritten artwork using Live Trace in Illustrator.

1 In your Lesson01 folder, double-click the file check_masthead_black.ai.

2 In Illustrator, select the Zoom tool (🔍) in the Tools panel, or press the Z key, and then click to zoom in close enough to scrutinize the outline of the logo in detail. Some of the unevenness you see along the edges can be smoothed out with the Blob Brush tool.

3 Before using the brush, first make sure the correct color for the check logo is active. The logo is filled with black and has no stroke. Select the Eyedropper tool (𝒻) in the Tools panel and click on the logo. The Color panel will display a black fill and no stroke.

4 In the Tools panel, double-click the Blob Brush tool (✎). When the Blob Brush Tool Options dialog box appears, choose Merge Only with Selection, drag the Fidelity slider to 3 pixels, and change the brush Size to 3 pt in the Default Brush Options. Then click OK.

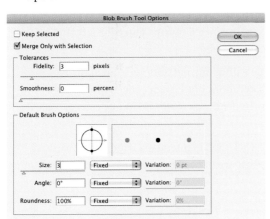

5   To demonstrate the refinements possible with the Blob Brush, let's have a closer look at the letter *e* in the check logo. Notice the dent in the lower-left side. With the Blob Brush still selected, add a few strokes to smooth the outline.

6   If you are not happy with the strokes you just painted with the Blob Brush tool, use the Eraser tool from the Tools panel to correct them—you can erase your strokes without ever breaking the outline.

7   Once you're happy with your refinements to the logo, select the Zoom tool (🔍), press the Alt/Option key for the Zoom Out mode, and then click on the logo to zoom out until you can see the entire document.

8   Choose File > Save As, navigate to your Lesson01 folder, name the file check_masthead_done.ai, and click Save. Then close the document.

Next, you'll take advantage of another great feature of Illustrator CS5: multiple artboards, which are like separate pages within one file. You'll create another artboard for a copy of the logo.

Setting up multiple artboards

● **Note:** During the process of creating a new Illustrator document you can specify the number of artboards you want and their size, position, and spacing in the New Document dialog box.

In Illustrator CS5 you can work with up to 100 different artboards in a single file. You have control of the size of the artboards as well as the spacing in between them. Multiple artboards can be named and organized in rows and columns, and can be printed, exported, and saved separately.

Being able to have several artboards within one file suits very much the way most designers work: Usually numerous iterations of a design concept are necessary to arrive at the polished final version. To help you create variations, you can quickly copy an object across all artboards.

1   In your Lesson01 folder, double-click the file InteractiveBanner_artboards.ai. This file contains five artboards that are to become pages of an interactive banner later in the book.

2 Choose Window > Artboards. In the Artboards panel, double-click Artboard 1. This is a quick way to zoom in on an artboard. You can use the Zoom tool and zoom out to see the entire canvas, which is quite large.

3 In the Tools panel, select the Artboard tool (), or press Shift+O. This tool enables you to manipulate the position of an artboard or change its size, and also create new artboards.

With the Artboard tool selected, handles appear around the current artboard and the area surrounding the artboard, called the canvas, becomes gray. You can use the handles to resize that artboard.

4 In the Options bar, enter **Future** as the new Name for the selected artboard.

5 In the Artboards panel, use the Move Down button to move the Future artboard to the bottom of the list, because the Future panel is supposed to be the last page in the interactive banner. Select the GuidePage artboard and use the Move Down button to move it into the third position.

6   Choose View > Fit All in Window so that you can see all artboards, and then choose Rearrange Artboards from the Artboards panel menu. Specify options as shown in the following illustration, and click OK.

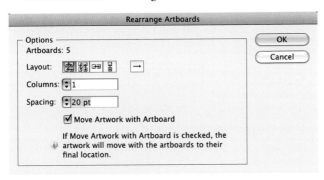

Drawing in perspective in Illustrator

When you want to use linear perspective to create depth in Illustrator CS5, it takes no time at all to set up a perspective grid. You can then forget about the technical points of perspective drawing and simply concentrate on your artwork.

1   In Illustrator, choose File > New, or if the Welcome screen is open, click Print Document in the Create New section. Click OK.

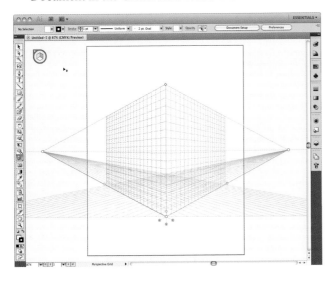

2 Select the Perspective Grid tool (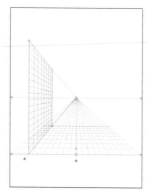). The perspective grid appears.

3 Try dragging the various perspective grid controls:

- The diamond-shaped handles at the bottom move the entire grid.

- The diamond-shaped handles at the far-left and far-right sides control the height of the horizon line.

- The circular handles on the left and right sides of the grid change the angles of each plane.

▶ **Tip:** You can save your own presets by choosing View > Perspective Grid > Save Grid as Preset.

4 Choose View > Perspective Grid > One-Point Perspective > -[1P-Normal View] to see a preset for one-point perspective. Then choose View > Perspective Grid > Three-Point Perspective > [3P-Normal View] to see a preset for three-point perspective.

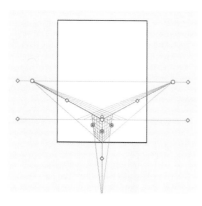

Now that you've seen how the perspective grid works, you can see it in action.

5   Close the current untitled document window without saving changes.

6   In your Lesson01 folder, double-click the file Perspective_Start.ai. If a Font Problems dialog box appears, click Open.

This is a building that was drawn using the perspective grid. Now you'll add a couple of windows to it.

7   Choose View > Windows. This brings you to the document view that was saved under the name Windows. With the Selection tool, select the second window in the top row, and then choose Edit > Copy.

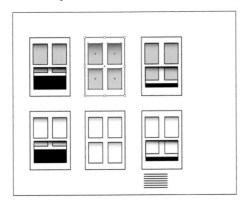

8   Choose View > Initial View.

9 In the plane switching widget, click the empty area outside the cube to make sure no perspective planes are selected, and then choose Edit > Paste.

10 In the Tools panel, select the Perspective Selection tool (). Click the right plane of the cube in the plane switching widget, and then drag the window you pasted into the empty area to the right of the upper window on the right face of the building.

11 Alt/Option-Shift-drag the selected window down to make a copy that lines up with the lower row of windows. As long as you drag with the Perspective Selection tool, the object follows the perspective of the selected plane.

Verifying your document's quality settings

Before saving graphics, it's a good idea to verify the quality of your document.

1 Choose Effect > Document Raster Effects Settings. When the Document Raster Effects Settings dialog box appears, change the default Screen Resolution (72 ppi) to High (300 ppi), and then click OK.

2   Choose File > Save As and save the document into your Lesson01 folder, naming the file **perspective.ai**. In the Illustrator Options dialog box, make sure the options Create PDF Compatible File, Embed ICC Profiles, and Use Compression are all selected, and then click OK.

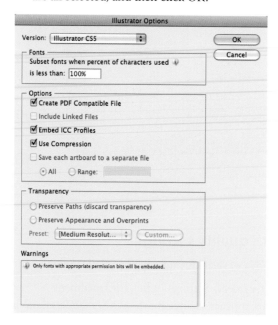

3   Close the file.

You've finished working on elements in Illustrator, which you'll use in later lessons. Next you'll experiment with the 3D features in Photoshop to create an asset you'll need for a Flash animation later on. Have fun!

Removing a background in Photoshop

Extracting a subject from a background is one of the most time-consuming tasks a designer faces. The most difficult part of this task is precisely masking out the edge, especially where hair or fur is involved. The new Truer Edge selection technology in Photoshop CS5 offers better edge detection and masking results in less time.

1 In your Lesson01 folder, double-click the file selection.psd to open it. In the Layers panel, select the Original layer.

2 Choose Select > Load Selection, select model selection from the Channel menu, and then click OK.

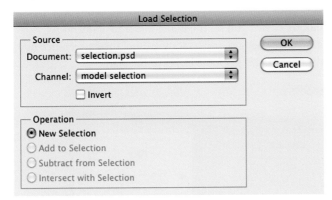

3 Choose any selection tool (such as the Rectangular Marquee tool), and then click Refine Edge in the Options bar.

4 Click the View icon and choose On Black to make the changes easier to see.

5 Select the Smart Radius check box and set the radius slider to about 30 px. Watch how the selection edge changes, particularly around the hair. Notice how the selection automatically changes from the jacket to fine hair.

6   In the Refine Edge dialog box, select the Refine Radius tool (). Drag along the hair edge near the woman's shoulder to extend the radius outward to include more of her hair. If you want to reduce the radius, Alt/Option-drag the Refine Radius tool along the outside of the selection.

7   Select Decontaminate Colors to remove colors from the original background that you don't want to show up against the new background.

8   Choose New Layer with Layer Mask from the Output To menu, and then click OK.

9 In the Layers panel, notice the new layer Original Copy and its mask. Click the eye icon for the Cityscape layer to display it, and notice how the subject is now composited with the cityscape seamlessly, including individual hairs.

10 Choose File > Save, name the document selection_done.psd, click Save.

Removing unwanted objects in Photoshop

Another traditionally time-consuming task is filling in areas where unwanted objects have been removed. This normally requires manually cloning and patching the empty area where the object used to be. In Photoshop CS5, Content-Aware Fill automatically matches lighting, tone, texture, and noise to make it look like the deleted area never existed.

1 In your Lesson01 folder, double-click the file content-aware.psd to open it. With the Lasso tool, make a rough selection just outside the man.

2 Press the Delete key. In the Fill dialog box, make sure Content-Aware is selected in the Use menu, and click OK.

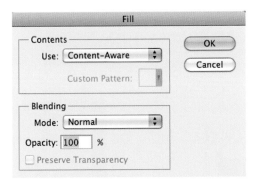

3 The man is deleted and filled in with the surrounding wall texture. Choose Select > Deselect to view the image without the selection.

4 Close the document and save your changes.

Another valuable use for Content-Aware Fill is in removing wires, graffiti, or other fine or thin objects. For this task it's better to use the Spot Healing Brush in Content-Aware mode.

5   In your Lesson01 folder, double-click the file content-aware_spot.psd to open it. Select the Spot Healing Brush, and in the Options bar, select the Content-Aware option.

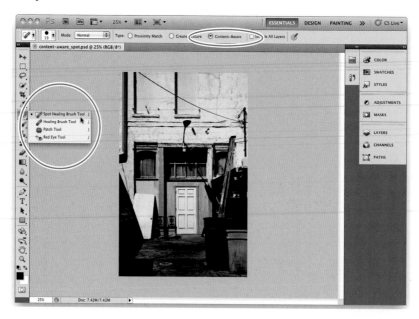

6   Drag the Spot Healing Brush along the wire at the top of the image. When you release the mouse, observe how the wire has been removed seamlessly because the surrounding textures and window frames have been detected and matched.

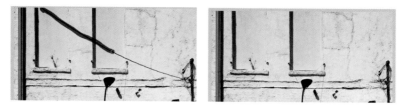

7   If you like, try removing other fixtures in the image. When you're done, close the document and save your changes.

Creating a 3D image in Photoshop

Photoshop CS5 Extended makes it easy to enhance your designs by creating 3D objects from 2D artwork using the new Adobe Repoussé feature—a fast, simple way to create 3D extrusions of any text layer, selection, path, or layer mask.

1 In your Lesson01 folder, double-click the file text_animation.psd to open it. Choose 3D from the workspace menu to switch to the 3D workspace.

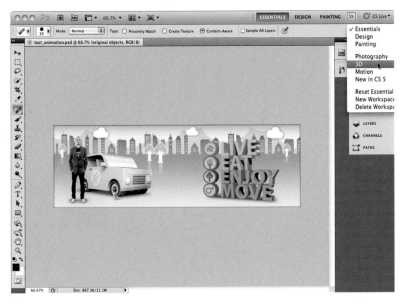

2 In the Layers panel, expand the original objects layer group and the original text layer group.

3 Alt/Option-click the eye icon for the MOVE layer to hide all other layers (including the other text layers) and then click the eye icon for the Background layer and the original objects layer group so that they are the only items visible.

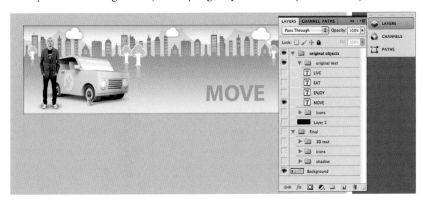

4 In the Layers panel, select the Move layer. In the document window, use the Move tool to drag the Move layer to the center of the image.

5 Choose Window > 3D. In the 3D panel, make sure that Selected Layer(s) is selected in the Source menu, select 3D Repoussé Object, and click Create. (If an alert appears warning about rasterization, click OK.)

6 Experiment by clicking on some of the Repoussé Shape Presets at the top of the dialog box, and observe how they change the Move layer in the document. When you're done, select the first preset.

7 In the Extrude section, adjust the Depth value to around 3. Explore the other options in the Extrude, Inflate, and Bevel sections. If you aren't sure what to do, you can use the settings in the following illustration.

While the Repoussé dialog box is open, you can drag inside the document window to rotate the object in 3D space. This is a good way to check your work.

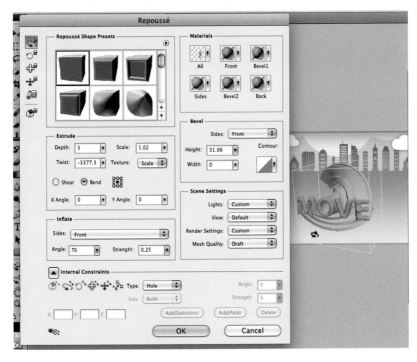

8   When you like your 3D model, click OK.

If you want to edit the 3D model, choose 3D > Repoussé > Edit in Repoussé.

You've created a true 3D model. You can use it with the 3D tools in Photoshop, paint on it, and animate it. If you want to see an example of what's possible with Repoussé 3D in Photoshop CS5 Extended, double-click the movie text_animation. mov in your Lesson01 folder.

In addition, you've learned many of the Adobe Creative Suite 5 Design Premium features that are important for preparing assets for projects. Throughout this book you'll see how assets you worked on in this lesson fit into larger workflows.

Review questions

1 How can you speed up the process of finding files and folders in Adobe Bridge?

2 Why would you use Adobe Bridge to synchronize your color settings when working within Adobe Creative Suite 5 applications?

3 What is so special about the Blob Brush tool in Adobe Illustrator CS5?

4 What are some practical uses for artboards?

5 How is Content-Aware Fill useful?

Review answers

1 Select a file or folder and choose File > Add to Favorites. The file or folder will appear in the Favorites panel in the left panel group of the Bridge window where you have easy access to it. Alternatively, you can drag the file or folder—or even an application— directly into the Favorites panel.

2 Adobe Bridge provides centralized access to your project files and enables you to synchronize color settings across all color-managed Creative Suite 5 applications. This synchronization ensures that colors look the same in all Adobe Creative Suite 5 components. If color settings are not synchronized, a warning message appears at the top of the Color Settings dialog box in each application. It is highly recommended that you synchronize color settings before starting to work with new or existing documents.

3 While sketching with the Blob Brush tool you can create a filled vector shape with a single outline, even when your strokes overlap. All the separate paths merge into a single object, which can easily be edited. You can customize the Blob Brush by specifying the stroke character and pressure sensitivity. Using the Blob Brush tool in combination with the Eraser tool enables you to make your shapes perfect—still keeping a single, smooth outline.

4 You can use artboards to organize related components of a project in a single Illustrator file, such as an envelope, business card, and letterhead; maintain multiple pages of an interactive online project; or store multiple versions of a project.

5 Content-Aware Fill saves time because it automatically fills in deleted objects by matching the lighting, tone, texture, and noise of surrounding areas instead of requiring you to manually patch the area.

2 CREATING A PRINT LAYOUT

Lesson Overview

In this lesson, you'll learn the skills and techniques you need to put together a sophisticated print magazine:

- Using Mini Bridge and Bridge to preview and select files
- Creating a document in InDesign
- Working with layer comps in Photoshop files
- Adjusting raw images
- Importing and styling text
- Laying out graphics efficiently
- Working with transparency

 You'll probably need between one and two hours to complete this lesson.

Quickly identify and import files iusing Bridge and Mini Bridge. Add text and graphics in a variety of file formats and take advantage of advanced layout tools. Then prepare your documents for high-quality printed output.

Inspecting and selecting documents with Adobe Bridge

If you've ever looked at a folder full of files and were unsure about which one you should open, take advantage of Adobe Bridge. Using Bridge to find the right document is often easier than using the standard Open dialog box, because Bridge gives you tools to inspect documents without opening them. Bridge can preview many file types produced in Design Premium. For InDesign files, Bridge can display the fonts and links in an InDesign document, and you can preview the document's pages.

You'll use Adobe Bridge to locate a partially completed InDesign document that you will use for the exercises in this lesson. The document represents the latest issue of a printed magazine.

1 Start Adobe Bridge, and make sure the Essentials workspace is selected at the top of the Bridge window.

2 Navigate to the Lesson02 folder on your hard disk. Within that folder, select the file Magazine_Start.indt.

3 In the Preview panel, click the arrow buttons under the document preview to explore the InDesign document without opening it.

4 Notice the chain link badge at the top-right corner of the selected InDesign document icon in the Content panel. This badge indicates that you can inspect the links in the InDesign document. You'll do that next.

5 Scroll the Metadata panel until you find the Linked Files pane, where you can view a list of the files linked to this InDesign document. Click the triangle icon to reveal the list.

Notice that above the Linked Files pane is the Fonts pane, where you can see which fonts are used in the InDesign document. Now you'll open the document.

Jump-starting design and production using templates

When you produce a certain type of document repeatedly, such as a monthly issue of a magazine, you can save time by starting each issue from a template. A template is an InDesign document that contains any custom design elements and production settings you save into it, such as master page layouts, background elements, placeholder frames for text and graphics, and text and object styles. When you open a template it opens as a new, untitled InDesign document. Using templates as the basis for frequently created documents is faster and easier than opening an old version and deleting all the content.

To create your own template from any InDesign document, choose File > Save As and then choose InDesign CS5 Template from the Format menu. Template documents used the .indt filename extension.

6   Select the file Magazine_Start.indt, and then choose File > Open With > Adobe InDesign CS5 (default).

Magazine_Start.indt is a template—it opens as a new, untitled document (see the sidebar "Jump-starting design and production using templates".) You'll save this document under a new name; the template file will remain unchanged so that you can always go back to it if you need to start over.

7   In InDesign, choose File > Save. In the Save As dialog box, navigate to the Lesson02 folder, name the document **Magazine.indd**, choose InDesign CS5 document from the Save As Type/Format menu, and then click Save.

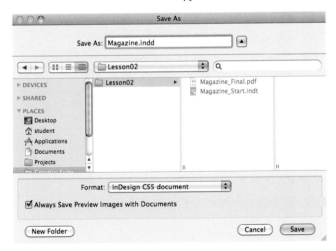

Modifying an InDesign document

Now that you have created a document from the InDesign template, you can adjust it just as you can any other InDesign document. You can replace illustrations and photos, add and stylize text, and even change the document layout settings you've acquired from the template.

Navigating through the document

Before making any changes to the document, navigate through its pages so you can plan which elements you'd like to customize.

▶ **Tip:** The visibility of menu items can be customized in InDesign. Selecting a predefined workspace may result in some menu items being hidden. If you can't find the menu item you're looking for, choose Show All Menu Items at the bottom of the menu, when available.

1 Choose Window > Workspace > [Advanced]. This will lay out all the panels you'll need for this lesson and make all menu commands visible.

2 Use the navigation buttons in the lower-left corner of your document window to navigate through the pages of the magazine. Then use the menu next to the current page number to return to the first page.

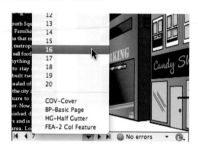

3 Click the Pages button in the right panel bin to open the Pages panel. If necessary, enlarge the Pages panel by dragging its lower-right corner downwards so you can see preview images of all pages. Double-clicking a page in the Pages panel will open that page in the main document window. Double-clicking the page number under the preview image will center the page spread in the main document window.

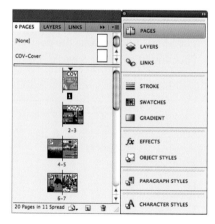

4 Click the Pages button in the right panel bin again to close the Pages panel.

Viewing the reference document

In the Lesson02 folder you'll find a PDF version of the completed magazine that you can use as a reference as you work through this lesson. This time we'll use Mini Bridge, a version of Adobe Bridge that you can use as a panel inside InDesign for easier access to the assets you want to bring into an InDesign document.

1 Choose Window > Mini Bridge. If you see a "Browse Files" icon, click it now.

2 Navigate to the Lesson02 folder, and select the file Magazine_Final.pdf in the Lesson02 folder.

3 Right-click/Control-click Magazine_Final.pdf, and choose Open.

4 In Acrobat, choose View > Page Display > Two-Up and View > Zoom > Fit Width. Then use the arrow keys on your keyboard to navigate through the spreads.

5 When you're done, return to InDesign. You can leave the PDF document open for reference.

Working with multiple page sizes

The magazine cover looks good, but to give it a little more interest, the client wants to extend the right side of the cover using a foldover flap. You'll create this by adding a page to the cover to create a spread. In addition, the page you add to the spread will use a smaller, narrow page size.

1   In the Pages panel, double-click page 1, then right-click/Control-click the Page 1 thumbnail, choose Insert Pages, and in the dialog box that appears, click OK.

Because you created the new page from Page 1, it's part of the Page 1 spread.

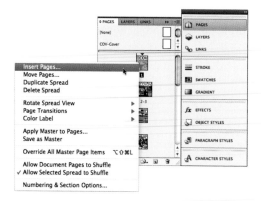

2   In the Tools panel, click the Page tool ( ), and then click the new page you created. As you do this, the Control panel displays options for the selected page.

3   In the Control panel, change the page width (W) to 18p6.

4   In the Layers panel, click the triangle to the left of the Text layer and Background Art layer to reveal sublayers and the objects on those layers.

5   Click the square icon to the right of the <Cover_Models.psd> object label to select it.

6 In the Tools panel, click the Selection tool (▶). Drag the handle in the middle of the right edge to extend the graphic all the way across the new page until the graphic is 93p1.6 wide, all the way to the right edge of the bleed area. The Control panel and the tool tip display the width as you drag.

▶ **Tip:** To adjust the bleed and slug areas, choose File > Document Setup. If you don't see the Bleed and Slug options, click the More Options button.

7 Choose Edit > Deselect All.

You could have also selected the graphic by clicking it with the Selection tool, but on a busy layout like this one, using the Layers panel can be a more direct way of ensuring that you select exactly the object you want.

Selecting and editing frames that are stacked behind other frames

The sunrise image should also be extended across the new page, but you can't select it by clicking because it's completely behind the Cover_Models.psd image. Fortunately, there's more than one way to select it.

▶ **Tip:** You can restack objects by dragging them up and down in the Layers panel.

1 With the Selection tool, hold down the Control/Command key, and then click the sunrise image. The first time you click, the bounding box for the Cover_Models.psd image may activate. Keep the Control/Command key pressed and click again until the blue outline of the sunrise image activates. You can confirm this by noting which object in the Layers panel has a selected square to the right of it.

2 Once the sunrise image's frame is selected, you can drag the handle in the middle of the right edge until it is 74 picas wide.

● **Note:** With multiple overlapping frames, you may need to Control/Command-click repeatedly through the stack until the correct frame is selected.

3 Save your changes.

The second way to select the sunrise image would be to locate it in the Layers panel and click the square to the right of it, as you did with the Cover_Models.psd image.

Placing a Photoshop file with layer comps

Navigate to the last page, the back cover. Currently, the back cover is blank. You will first place the back page photo into the frame provided for it, and then make adjustments to the image in Photoshop.

1 Use the Selection tool to select the frame on the last page.

● **Note:** If your placed graphic does not look as smooth as shown in the illustration on this page, choose View > Display Performance > High Quality Display.

2 Choose File > Place. Navigate to the Links folder inside the Lesson02 folder. Select the file wifi_laptop.psd, select both Show Import Options and Replace Selected Items, and then click Open.

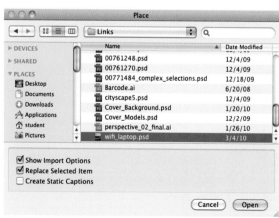

3   In the Image Import Options (wifi_laptop.psd) dialog box, select the Show
    Preview option. In the Layers tab, notice that not all layers are turned on.
    Choose Sponsor Off from the Layer Comp menu; the preview thumbnail
    updates. Click OK.

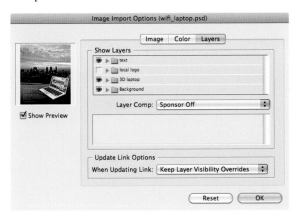

4   To view the cover without page frames and guide lines, click the Screen Mode
    button at the bottom of the Tools panel and choose Preview. When you're done
    previewing, choose Normal from the same menu. You can also toggle between
    Normal and Preview by pressing the W key.

▶ **Tip:** You can hide
or show each layer
independently. Layer
comps are just a
convenient way to hide
or show preselected
groups of layers.

The sunset doesn't match the blue bottom background very well, so you will now
use Photoshop to unify the image by altering the color balance of the sky.

5   Use the Selection tool to select the frame containing the image and choose
    Edit > Edit With > Adobe Photoshop CS5 (default).

6 In the Layers panel in Photoshop, click the triangle next to the Background layer group to reveal its contents. Select the Background Image layer at the bottom of the Layers panel.

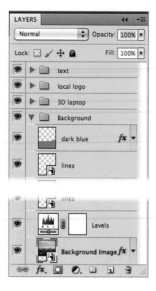

7 In the Adjustments panel, click the Color Balance icon. This adds a new Color Balance adjustment layer immediately above the selected layer.

8 In the Color Balance panel, make sure Midtones is selected, and then enter **-62** for the Cyan/Red slider, **1** for the Magenta/Green slider, and **31** for the Red/Blue slider. Leave Preserve Luminosity selected.

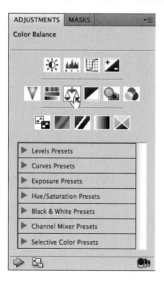 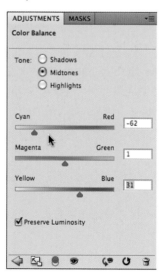

Because the document now contains a layer that wasn't included in the original layer comps, you'll learn how to update the layer comps so they're properly preserved when you return to InDesign.

9 Open the Layer Comps panel (Window > Layer Comps). Two layer comps have already been defined, named Sponsor Off and Sponsor On. Click the box to the left of the Sponsor On layer name to enable that layer comp, and notice the effect it has on the visibility of the layers in the Layers panel and in the image.

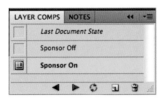

A layer comp is simply a snapshot of the visibility, position, and layer style settings for various layers in the Layers panel. You may notice that the Color Balance layer you created was turned off when you turned on the Sponsor On layer comp, because that layer didn't exist when the layer comp was originally saved.

10 Turn on the Color Balance layer, make sure Sponsor On is highlighted in the Layer Comps panel (but don't turn it on), and then choose Update Layer Comp from the Layer Comps panel menu. Now the Sponsor On layer comp includes the Color Balance adjustment layer. You can repeat this process for the Sponsor Off layer comp: Turn on the layer comp, turn on the Color Balance adjustment layer, and update the layer comp.

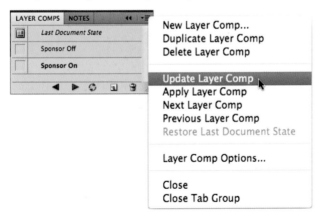

When placing a Photoshop file containing layer comps in InDesign, you can choose which version—or layer comp—you want to use in your publication without having to reopen and adjust the file in Photoshop.

11 Save changes, close the document, and then switch back to InDesign. An alert may appear, letting you know that the graphic has changed, click OK.

12 With the back cover image still selected in InDesign, choose Object > Object Layer Options. From the Layer Comp menu in the Object Layer Options dialog box, choose Sponsor On, select the Preview check box to see the effect, and then click OK.

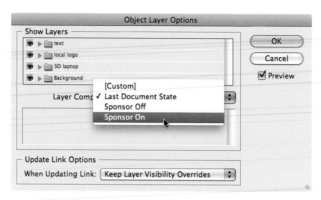

Working with camera raw images

● **Note:** Camera raw is not a single format. Each camera sensor model may have a different raw format and filename extension. Most camera raw formats can be converted to the DNG (Adobe Digital Negative) format.

Camera raw format files are now common for high-quality digital photographs. The Camera Raw plug-in for Adobe Photoshop enables you to adjust a raw image and to then save it in a file format that can be placed in InDesign.

1 In InDesign, navigate to page 17. If not already selected, choose View > Screen Mode > Normal. If you don't see guidelines on the page, choose View > Grids & Guides > Show Guides.

2 Select the empty graphics frame on page 17 and choose Object > Fitting > Frame Fitting Options. Select Auto-Fit, choose Fill Frame Proportionally, and click the center of the Align From proxy. These options ensure that no matter the size of the image, it will be sized to fit the frame and centered within it, saving you time in fitting the image to the frame.

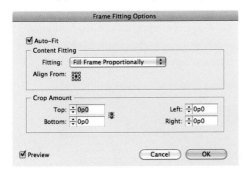

3 In the Mini Bridge panel (Window > Mini Bridge), navigate to the Lesson02 folder. Double-click the raw image file named coffee_cup.dng. The image will open in Photoshop in the Camera Raw dialog box.

▶ **Tip:** For detailed information about digital camera raw file support in Photoshop, refer to www.adobe.com/products/photoshop/cameraraw.html.

4   To adjust the white balance in a camera raw image, you can choose from a predefined setting or pick a reference area within the image. Explore the different settings in the White Balance menu in the Basic panel and note the effect on the image colors. To adjust the color relative to an area in the image that should be a neutral mid-gray, select the White Balance tool from the Tools panel and then click inside the reference area. Clicking the White Balance tool on the coffee cup neutralizes the image colors. However, this photo is intended to convey a warm coffee-shop atmosphere, so restore the original white balance by choosing As Shot from the White Balance menu.

5   The image is a little flat, so it could use more contrast. To have Camera Raw determine a starting point for correction, click the underlined Auto text. From this point you can refine the automatic correction by dragging the sliders. The image is a little dark now, so increase the Brightness value to around 33.

6 To specify a fixed aspect ratio for the Crop tool, click and hold the Crop tool
   button in the toolbar, and then select an aspect ratio from the menu. We chose
   4 to 5 to approximate the proportions of the frame in the InDesign layout, with
   a little room to spare.

7 Using the Crop tool, drag across the image to create a crop rectangle, as shown
   in the illustration.

At this point you could click Open Image to open the image in Photoshop and make further adjustments if necessary. For this exercise, you'll just save the file in a format that can be used in InDesign.

8   Click the Save Image button in the lower-left corner of the Camera Raw dialog box. In the Save Options dialog box, choose Save in New Location from the Destination menu, and select the Links folder inside the Lesson02 folder as the destination for the saved file. Type **_cropped** to add it to the document name, select Photoshop for the file format, and then click Save.

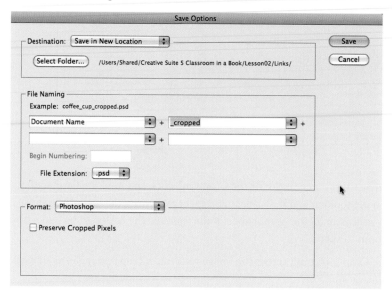

9   Click Done to close the Camera Raw dialog box and return to InDesign.

10 In InDesign, use Mini Bridge to navigate to the Links folder inside the Lesson02 folder. Drag the file coffee_cup_cropped.psd and drop it into the empty frame on page 17. The coffee cup image is automatically sized within and centered in the frame because of the Auto Fit settings you applied in step 2.

11 With the frame selected, notice the Content Grabber in the middle of the image. Drag this indicator to move the image within the frame. The Content Grabber lets you adjust the position of the image within the frame without having to select a separate tool.

12 Save your changes.

Importing and styling text

You can enter text directly into an InDesign document by typing into the text frames. For longer text passages, however, it is more common to import text from an external text document. You can style the text as part of the import process or manually change the text appearance later.

1   In InDesign, navigate to page 12 of the magazine document.

The text columns of the feature story are filled with placeholder text. You'll replace the placeholder text with text from a Word document.

2   Select the Type tool in the Tools panel and place the cursor anywhere in the text in the two main text columns on page 12. Choose Edit > Select All. The text in both columns is selected because the text columns are linked. These text frames are also linked with the text frames on the next few pages.

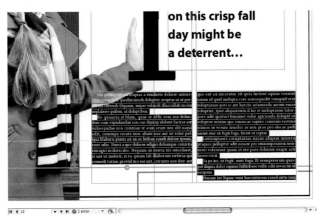

3   Choose File > Place. In the Place dialog box, navigate to the Lesson02 folder, select the file Main_Story.doc, select both Show Import Options and Replace Selected Item, and click Open.

4   Under Formatting in the Microsoft Word Import Options (Main_Story.doc) dialog box, select Preserve Styles And Formatting From Text And Tables, and Customize Style Import. Click the Style Mapping button.

The Style Mapping dialog box enables you to match type styles defined in the Word document to type styles defined in the InDesign document. If you set up the styles with identical names, InDesign can perform the mapping automatically.

In this case, the Style Mapping dialog box shows that the Microsoft Word style Sidebar Bullet List doesn't match up with any style names in InDesign, so you'll have to map this style manually.

5   In the InDesign Style column in the Style Mapping dialog box, click [New Paragraph Style] to the right of the Microsoft Word style Sidebar Bullet List, and choose Sidebar Bulleted List. This maps the Word style to the InDesign style, which in this case is correct because the two styles are actually the same, but were named slightly differently in the two programs.

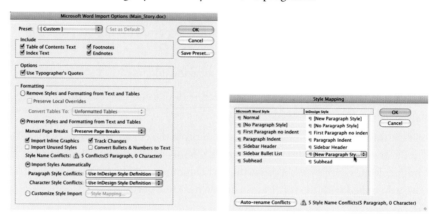

6   Click OK to close the Style Mapping dialog box, and then click OK to close the Import Options dialog box.

The imported text replaces the text in the two text frames and in the threaded text frames in the pages that follow, and the styles in the text take on the formatting defined by the same style names in InDesign. The text on page 12 overlaps the woman's arm; you'll fix that a little later.

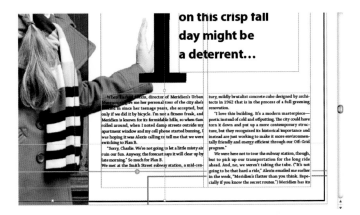

7   Navigate to page 13 to see how the story continues through the threaded frames to the next spread.

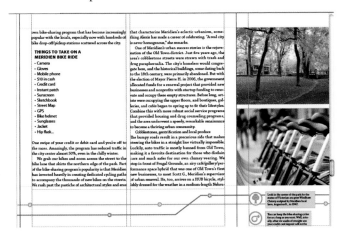

Applying paragraph styles

In the story you just imported, one of the headings has the wrong style applied. It's body text, but it should be a heading. You'll fix this by applying the correct paragraph style.

1   While viewing page 13, open the Paragraph Styles panel (Window > Styles > Paragraph Styles).

2   Select the Text tool from the Tools panel and click to place the flashing cursor inside the heading "Cobblestones, gentrification and local produce". For a paragraph style, it is not necessary to select the entire paragraph.

3 In the Paragraph Styles panel, select the Subhead paragraph style. Notice the change in the text in the document window.

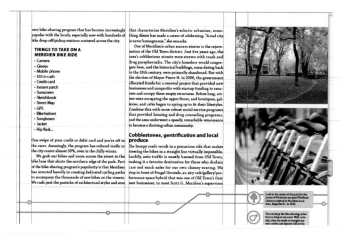

4 Save your changes.

Wrapping text around frames

Now that the text is formatted properly, it's time to take care of the text overlapping the woman's arm on page 12.

1 With the Selection tool, click the woman's arm.

While not currently visible, this image contains a clipping path that was drawn in Adobe Photoshop to cut the image out of its red background. You can also use this path as a text wrap boundary.

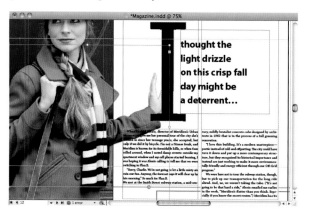

2 In the Text Wrap panel (Window > Text Wrap), click the third button from the left in the top row. This button wraps text around the shape of the object's frame.

3 In the Text Wrap panel, choose Photoshop Path from the Contour Options: Type menu. There is only one clipping path stored in the document, Path 1, which appears in the Path menu. The clipping path is now used as the frame for the image, hiding all parts of the image that lie outside the frame path.

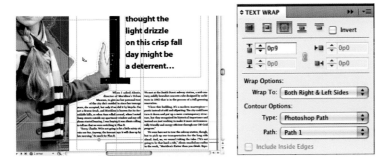

Note that a 9-point wrap offset distance is specified in the Text Wrap panel. You can adjust this number to control the distance of the text wrap from the object frame, but you don't need to make an adjustment here.

If you wanted to edit the shape of the object frame, you could select the Direct Selection tool to move the points on the frame.

Splitting paragraphs within columns and spanning paragraphs across columns

There's some additional layout work to be done on page 13. To improve the composition of the page, you'll change the two columns on the page to three columns, and you'll convert some of the text into a sidebar. Fortunately, this will be as simple as selecting text and choosing options in the Control panel.

1 Go to page 13, and with the Selection tool, click the two-column text frame.

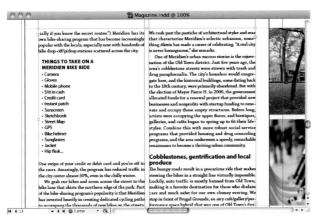

2 Choose Object > Text Frame Options, change the Number of columns to 3, and click OK.

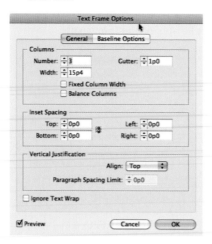

3 With the Type tool, select the bullet list in the first column. (Don't select the heading.)

4 Make sure the Control panel is in Paragraph Formatting mode (the paragraph symbol is selected at the left edge), and choose Split 2 from the Span Columns menu in the Control panel.

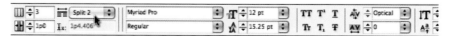

5   Click the Type tool in the "Cobblestones, gentrification…" heading and choose
    Span 2 from the same Span Columns menu in the Control panel.

6   In the Layers panel, if necessary click the triangle next to the Text layer to
    expand it. Then click in the eye column for the Blue Box object to make it visible
    behind the sidebar. The box was added by the designer to accommodate the
    sidebar.

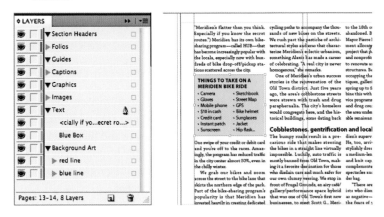

Laying out multiple photos in a grid

You can quickly and easily lay out many photos at once for publications such as
catalogs and yearbooks. InDesign simplifies and accelerates this process by letting
you place multiple photos into a grid you create as you import the images and by
using metadata inside images to generate automatic image captions on the layout.

1   Go to page 15, and in the Layers panel, select the layer Graphics. This ensures
    that images you import into InDesign will be placed on the Graphics layer.

2 In Mini Bridge, navigate to the Links folder. Select the four files 01_Fruitstand.psd, 02_Berries.psd, 03_Corn.psd, and 04_Flowers.psd, and drag all four selected items to page 15 of the InDesign layout.

3 Position the loaded Place cursor at the intersection of the left margin and the cyan guide below the text frame on page 15. Begin dragging, and while the mouse button is still down, press the Right Arrow key once and then the Up Arrow once to create a 2 x 2 grid. Continue dragging to the bottom-right corner of the page to the intersection of the lower ruler guide and the right margin guide, and then release the mouse. Leave the images selected.

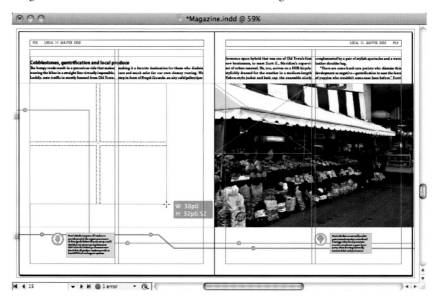

The images are set to fit within their frames, but you want these images to fill their frames while maintaining their proportions.

4   Choose Object > Fitting > Frame Fitting Options. In the dialog box, select Fill Frame Proportionally in the Fitting menu, and then select the center point in the Align From proxy. Click OK.

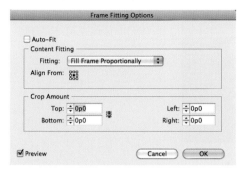

Creating live captions

Keywords, captions, and other metadata are becoming increasingly critical to print and online publishing. One way you can use metadata to enhance your publishing workflow is to automatically generate captions next to photos on the layout.

1   Choose Object > Captions > Caption Setup.

2   In the Caption Setup dialog box, set the first Metadata menu to Description. The other items in the menu are all forms of metadata that can potentially be included in an image by entering it using an application such as Adobe Bridge, or as shot data added by a camera.

3   If you see a second Metadata Caption line, click the minus sign after the end of the line to remove it.

4   In the Position and Style section, set the Offset to 1p0, choose Captions from the Paragraph Style menu, and then choose Captions from the Layer menu. Click OK.

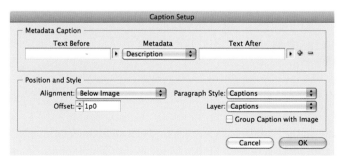

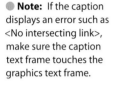
5   Use the Selection tool to select the image of the market on page 16. Zoom in to the bottom-left corner of the market image.

6   Choose Object > Captions > Generate Live Caption, and watch a caption appear to the specifications you set up in the Caption Setup dialog box.

This is a live caption because if the image description is changed (for example, using the Metadata panel in Adobe Bridge or Photoshop) when the image is updated in InDesign, the caption will update automatically.

Shortcuts for editing objects

Repetitive layout tasks such as aligning and distributing objects or customizing frame corners is easy and quick in InDesign CS5. You saw an example of this earlier when you used the Content Grabber to recompose an image inside a frame. You can take advantage of other layout tricks InDesign CS5.

1   Select the coffee cup image on page 16, and drag a corner of its frame to make the frame smaller. Notice that the image inside the frame resizes as well. This is a new optional setting in InDesign CS5.

2   With the image still selected, deselect the Auto Fit check box in the Control panel, and drag the corner of the image frame to enlarge it. This time the image doesn't scale with the frame. Choose Edit > Undo Resize Item, select Auto Fit, and drag the corner to enlarge the frame back to its original size. Then deselect the image.

You control how Auto Fit works in the same Frame Fitting Options dialog box you worked with earlier.

3   On page 15, hold down the Shift key as you click to select all of the four images you placed into a grid. Make sure Auto Fit is selected in the Control panel.

4   In the Layers panel, click in the eye column to hide the Background Art layer.

5 Select the Gap tool in the Tools panel, and then position it in the gap between any two of the four images. You may want to zoom in so that the gaps are larger.

6 Drag the Gap tool to control the space between the frames.

7 Shift-drag the Gap tool to adjust only the gap nearest the cursor. Each modifier key changes how the Gap tool works, so experiment with holding down the Alt/Option and Control/Command keys as you drag the Gap tool.

Now you'll use the Gap tool temporarily, using a feature called spring-loaded cursors. It's a quick way to use different tools with fewer trips to the Tools panel. Spring-loaded cursors take advantage of another time-saver: shortcut keys for tools. U is the shortcut key for the Gap tool.

8 Click the Selection tool in the Tools panel. This is the tool you'll probably be using most of the time.

9 Position the Selection tool over a gap between images, and then press and hold the U key. Notice that the cursor changes to the Gap tool; continue to hold down the U key as you drag to adjust the gap between the images. Release the U key and notice that the cursor returns to the Selection tool.

▶ **Tip:** To learn the shortcut keys, hold the cursor over various tools in the Tools panel until their tool tips appear; shortcut keys are listed in the tool tips.

Normally, pressing a shortcut key permanently switches tools. Spring-loading the cursor lets the new tool snap back to the old tool as soon as you release a shortcut key. Think of the difference this way: To use a shortcut key, briefly tap it; to use a shortcut key as a spring-loaded shortcut, hold it down until you're done.

10 With the Selection tool, click the image of berries, and then click the yellow control near the top-right corner of the image. The frame handles at the corners turn into diamond handles. These diamond handles let you customize the shapes of the frame corners.

Note: If you don't see the yellow handles, choose View > Extras > Show Live Corners. Also, make sure View > Screen Mode is set to Normal.

11 Drag any of the yellow diamond handles to adjust the corner radius of all corners. The corner radius value appears in the Corner Options section of the Control panel; choose a corner shape from the Corner Shape menu below the radius value. Shift-drag a diamond handle to adjust just one corner, or Alt/ Option-click a diamond handle to change the corner shape.

Tip: Alt/Option-click the Corner Options icon in the Control panel to open the Corner Options dialog box.

Note: If you don't see the yellow handles, choose View > Extras > Show Live Corners. Also, make sure View > Screen Mode is set to Normal.

Tip: Another way to change corner shapes is to Alt/Option-drag a corner handle.

12 In the Layers panel, click in the eye column for the Background Art layer to make that layer visible again.

Tracking text changes

Get to final copy faster by tracking text changes directly in your InDesign document. You can write, edit, and mark up text in InDesign CS5 without needing to import separate text files and remap styles every time there are copy changes.

1 Navigate to page 13. Choose Window > Editorial > Assignments, and then choose User from the Assignments panel menu. Enter a User Name, choose a Color, and click OK.

2 With the Type tool, click to place an insertion point inside the text story. Choose Window > Editorial > Track Changes. The top-left button in the Track Changes panel controls whether change tracking is enabled, and the next button controls whether changes are visible. Make sure both buttons are on.

3 In the "Things to Take on a Meridien Bike Ride" sidebar, select the text *10* and type **25**.

4 Choose Edit > Edit in Story Editor to open the Story Editor display and note the highlight color. Click in the highlighted text and notice that the Track Changes panel indicates that you are the user who edited the text.

If you see text highlighted in other colors, that's text edited by other users whom you can identify in the Track Changes panel.

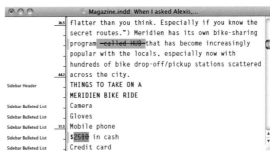

5   Click inside the highlighted text you edited and click the Accept Change button in the Track Changes panel.

6   When you're done, close the Story Editor window and the Track Changes panel.

Getting review feedback

● **Note:** CS Live online services are complimentary for a limited time. See page 25 for details and limitations related to all Adobe online services.

▶ **Tip:** Another way to start a review is by choosing File > Create New Review.

● **Note:** If you're using CS Live services for the first time, you may be asked to review and accept the terms of use for the services before you continue.

Using CS Review, an Adobe CS Live online service, you can create and share documents for online review without leaving InDesign. Colleagues and clients can view your document online and add comments directly using easy-to-use annotation tools that appear in their browsers. All comments appear within the context of your InDesign page layout. Simple sharing, easy access to reviews, and centralized comments speed up the review process so that you can finish your project on time and within budget.

To do this part of the lesson, make sure you've already set up an account on Acrobat.com.

1   Click the CS Live button at the top-right corner of the screen, and choose Create New Review. Enter a review name and click OK. (If you don't see the CS Live button, choose View > Application Bar.) You can also choose File > Create New Review. If you have not already signed into CS Live services, you may be asked to do so now."

2   In the Create New Review dialog box, the name of the document appears as the default Review Name. Add the words final draft to enter the complete review name Magazine_online Final Draft. If you are asked if you want to save the files, click Save

3   In the Upload Settings dialog box, make sure Current Spread (13-14) is selected. Leave the other settings as shown, and click Upload. These settings control how much of the document is made available on the server for the review, and the quality of the display for the reviewers.

After you click Upload, the CS Review panel displays upload progress. You'll use the CS Review panel to set up and monitor the review from within InDesign.

4   In the CS Review panel, click the View the current Review online button to display the review on Acrobat.com as your reviewers will see it. CS Review opens the document in your default web browser. To review the document, your reviewers only need a web browser running Flash; they don't need InDesign.

▶ **Tip:** To notify all of your reviewers about the review, simply click the Share button at the bottom of the CS Review panel.

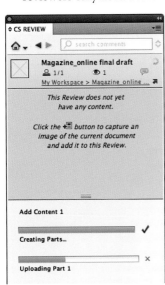

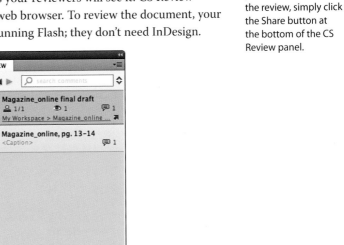

Now you'll make a couple of comments as if you were a reviewer.

5 On the Acrobat.com page in your Web browser, Acrobat.com displays the pages you made available. You can use the zoom buttons and the page navigator proxy to inspect the pages. Drag the mouse around the orange box at the bottom of page 14, the right page in the spread.

6 A comment box opens. Enter the text Is this too close to the bottom of the page?, and click Save. The comment appears on the right side of the review web page.

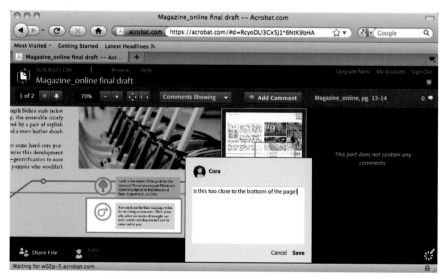

7 Position the mouse over the text near the lower-left corner of page 12. Notice that the cursor changes to a text cursor. Select the word shoulders at the end of the second-to-last paragraph on page 12 as shown.

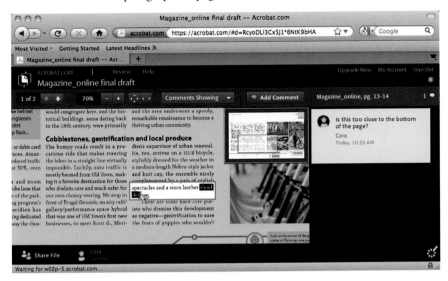

Notice that you can use CS Review to add comments for specific text passages as well as on the layout.

8 In the comment box that appears, enter Don't break this word, and click Save.

Now that you've made a couple of review comments, take a look at how you would see them as the InDesign user.

▶ **Tip:** Right-click/
Control-click items in
the CS Review panel
to see a context menu
with commands for
viewing and managing
comments.

9 Switch to InDesign and then click Magazine_online, pg. 13-14. In the CS Review panel, notice that the comments made online now appear in the CS Review pane. Comments made by any reviewer will appear here. You can then act on the comments as needed.

10 You're done exploring CS Review, so close the CS Review panel.

Preparing for printing

You've completed the design of the magazine. Since the document contains transparency effects, there are a few more adjustments necessary to get the best print results.

Transparent areas in a document need to be flattened—or rasterized—when printed. For best results, flattening should be done as the last possible step in your print workflow—normally performed by your print service provider. To keep transparency effects live until they need to be flattened, preserve the layers by saving your InDesign documents (or placed Illustrator or Photoshop files) in a native format.

You can help minimize the effects of flattening if you send your document output to devices that support the latest versions of PDF. To preserve transparency effects rather than flattening them when exporting a document as a PDF intended for printing, save your file in a format compatible with Adobe PDF 1.5 (Acrobat 5.0) or later—by selecting the PDF/X-4 PDF export preset, for example. The Adobe PDF Print Engine (APPE)—widely embraced by OEM partners and print service providers since first released in 2006 and updated to version 2 in 2008—uses native rasterizing for PDF documents, ensuring file integrity from start to finish in a PDF-based design workflow. To learn more about the Adobe PDF Print Engine, go to www.adobe.com/products/pdfprintengine.

In InDesign, the Flattener Preview panel helps you identify which areas will be most affected by the flattening process. You'll take a look at how that works.

Previewing how transparency will affect output

1   In InDesign, navigate to page 8 of the magazine document.

● **Note:** If the backgrounds of the text frames display as solid white on your screen, choose View > Display Performance > High Quality Display. If you still don't see the transparency, check your view settings preferences (in the Display Performance panel of the Preferences dialog box); set transparency to be rendered at high quality for your display performance mode. Your preferences for the display performance have no effect on how transparency is rendered when exported or printed.

2   To see which areas of your document are affected by transparency effects, open the Flattener Preview panel (Window > Output > Flattener Preview), select Transparent Objects from the Highlight menu, and choose [High Resolution] from the Preset menu. Then choose in turn in the Highlight menu: All Affected Objects, Affected Graphics, and All Rasterized Regions. When you're done, choose Transparent Objects.

The areas affected by each Highlight option are highlighted in red, such as the text frame in the lower-right corner of the page. You can use the Effects panel to find out why that object is highlighted. Specifically, you're looking for a blend mode other than Normal in the menu at the top of the Effects panel, an Opacity lower than 100%, or an applied effect.

3   Using the Selection tool, click the text frame. In the Effects panel (Window > Effects), note that it says Group and indicates no transparency. This means the transparency is probably applied to an object in the group.

4   Double-click the group to select the frame inside the group. Now that the text frame is selected, the Effects panel reveals that the Fill uses the Multiply blend mode and is set to 85% Opacity. These are the options that create transparency in this object.

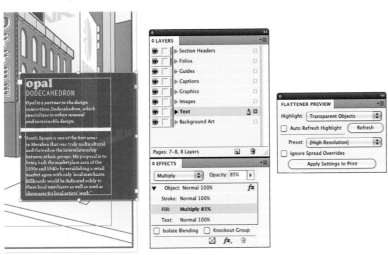

If the Flattener Preview panel reveals potential issues with how transparency will affect part of your document during output, you can decide what to do about those issues. For example, if you see that type or highly detailed vector graphics will become rasterized, you might decide to change the design to avoid the problem by moving critical objects so that they don't overlap objects that use transparency, or by avoiding the use of transparency in that area.

One thing to watch out for is text placed behind objects with transparency effects. Transparency affects all objects placed lower—or farther back—in the display stacking order. Printed text might not look as crisp as it should if it was converted to outlines and rasterized behind an object with a transparency effect, so when possible, it's best to keep text in front of transparent objects in the layer order.

If you need to flatten your document as part of the export or print process, for best results set the document's transparency blend space (Edit > Transparency Blend Space) to the color space (CMYK or RGB) of the target output device. For more information about working with transparency see "Best practices when creating transparency" in InDesign Help.

Checking the effective resolution of linked images

You can use the Links panel to verify that the linked images have a high enough resolution for your intended mode of output. The effective resolution of a placed image is defined by the resolution of the original image and the scale factor at which it is placed in InDesign. For example, an image with a 300 ppi (pixels per inch) resolution only has an effective resolution of 150 ppi when it's scaled to 200%.

For images to be viewed at screen resolution—published on a website or in a low resolution PDF document, for example—an effective resolution of 72 ppi is sufficient. For desktop printing, the effective resolution should be between 72 ppi and 150 ppi. For commercial printing your images should have an effective resolution between 150 ppi and 300 ppi (or higher), depending on the requirements of your prepress service provider.

1 In InDesign, open the Links panel. Choose Panel Options from the panel options menu. In the Panel Options dialog box, select the Actual PPI, Effective PPI, and Scale options in the Show column. Click OK to close the Panel Options dialog box. If necessary, resize the Links panel so that you can see the additional columns.

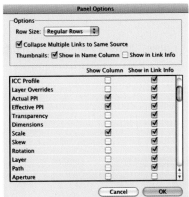

2 For each image placed in your document, check the actual resolution, the effective resolution, and the scale factor. For example, the cover image on page 1 has an actual resolution of 150 ppi but an effective resolution of 153 ppi because it was scaled by 98.2%. If a higher effective resolution is required for your print job, you could reduce the scale factor, which would show more of the image background, reduce the dimensions of the placed image—not really an option for the cover photo, which needs to cover the entire page—or select an image with a higher actual resolution—perhaps a close-up photo of the face rather than the wider shot that is used in this example.

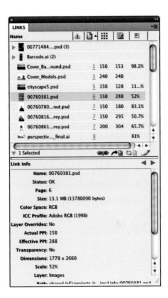

3 Close the Links panel.

Performing a preflight check

Rather than painstakingly checking through a list of possible problem areas each time you want to print or export a document, you can rely on InDesign to do all the work for you.

1   Choose Window > Output > Preflight. When the On check box is selected in the Preflight panel, InDesign continuously checks for possible problems while you're working on your document.

You can set up a preflight profile to specify which potential problems you want InDesign to look out for.

2   To define a preflight profile, choose Define Profiles from the Preflight panel options menu or from the Preflight menu located near the lower-left corner of the document window.

3   In the Preflight Profiles dialog box, click the Add button (⊕) below the list of profiles to create a new profile. Name the new profile **Resolution Check**. Activate the Image Resolution option inside the IMAGES and OBJECTS folder. Leave the Image Color Minimal Resolution set at 250 ppi, and then click OK.

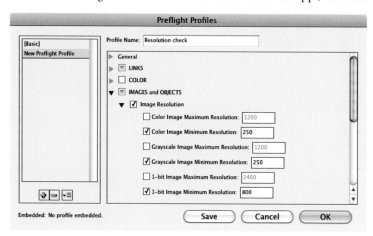

4   From the Profile menu in the Preflight panel, choose Resolution Check. If necessary, click the disclosure triangles next to the Images and Objects heading and the Info heading to expand their lists. InDesign finds several placed images that don't meet the set requirements. To review an error found by the Preflight check, click the page link in the Preflight panel. InDesign selects and jumps to the object causing the error. A description of the error and suggestions on how to fix the problem are provided in the Info section of the Preflight panel.

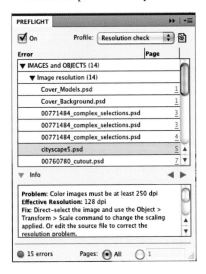

5   Switch back to the previous preflight profile by choosing [Basic] from the Profile menu in the Preflight panel, and then close the Preflight panel.

6   Save your document.

Exporting to PDF

Exporting your document as a PDF file enables you to preserve the look and feel of your InDesign document in a device independent format that can be viewed onscreen or printed on any printer. This can be particularly useful when you want to print a quick draft of your document on an inkjet printer at home or in your office. You can tweak the export settings, balancing quality and file size to create a PDF that is optimized to suit its intended purpose.

1   Choose File > Export. In the Export dialog box, navigate to the Lesson02 folder. From the Save As Type/Format menu, choose Adobe PDF Print; then, name the file **Magazine_Print.pdf** and click Save.

2   In the Export Adobe PDF dialog box, choose [High Quality Print] from the Adobe PDF Preset menu. Review—but don't change—the settings for this export preset in the various panels of the dialog box, and then click Export.

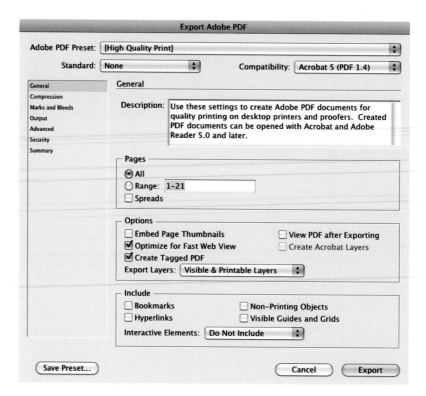

3   Open the Lesson02 folder in Windows Explorer/the Finder. Right-click/Control-
    click the file Magazine_Print.pdf and choose Open With > Adobe Acrobat Pro.

4   Use the page navigation controls in Acrobat to review the pages of the
    magazine. Pay special attention to the position and quality of the images
    you placed, the text styles you've adjusted, and the areas containing
    transparency effects.

5   When you're done reviewing, close the document in Acrobat and switch back
    to InDesign.

Review questions

1 How can you select a frame that is stacked behind another in an InDesign document?

2 How do you edit a page so that it's a different size than the rest of the document?

3 What is a layer comp?

4 What is the effective resolution of an image placed in InDesign?

5 What is the advantage of creating a preflight profile?

Review answers

1 To select a frame that is stacked behind another frame, hold down the Control/ Command key, and then click inside the frame you want to select. With multiple overlapping frames you may need to click repeatedly until the correct frame is selected. You can also select the topmost frame, and then choose Object > Select > Next Object Below.

2 With the Page tool, select the page you want to modify, and then edit the page dimensions in the Control panel.

3 A layer comp is a snapshot of the visibility settings of layers in a Photoshop document that can be used to organize multiple versions of a design in a single document. When placed in InDesign, you can quickly switch between the layer comps using the Object Layer Options dialog box.

4 The effective resolution of a placed image is defined by the actual resolution of the original image and the scale factor when placed in InDesign. For example, an image with a 300 ppi (pixels per inch) resolution has an effective resolution of only 150 ppi when scaled to 200%. Documents intended for print require images with a higher effective resolution than documents to be viewed only onscreen.

5 A preflight profile represents the output requirements of a specific job. When you create your own preflight profile that's tailored to the requirements of your print service provider, InDesign can continuously check the state of the document and its assets, and alert you to any problems that may cause an issue at output time. Because problems at output time can be expensive to fix, catching problems early can save you time and money.

3 CREATING AN ONLINE VERSION OF A PRINT LAYOUT

Lesson Overview

In this lesson, you'll learn all the skills and techniques you need to put together a sophisticated multimedia brochure:

- Adding animation

- Adding interactivity

- Editing movie files in Photoshop

- Adding video and audio

- Exporting to Flash Player and Flash Professional CS5 format

 You'll probably need between one and two hours to complete this lesson.

Learn how to easily add interactive elements to a print document for onscreen viewing, so that you can concentrate on design. Engage and inform readers and clients with documents and presentations that integrate interactivity, animation, sound, and video. Reduce costs by creating interactivity directly in InDesign. Decrease your carbon footprint by offering compelling online experiences that require no paper, ink, or shipping.

● **Note:** Before you start working on this lesson, make sure that you've installed the Creative Suite 5 Design Premium software on your computer, and that you have correctly copied the Lessons folder from the CD in the back of this book onto your computer's hard disk (see "Copying the Classroom in a Book files" on page 2).

About converting print documents to Flash

The City Guide document you'll use in this lesson starts out as an insert in the Local print magazine you've worked with in the earlier lessons. Converting the City Guide is straightforward because it was designed to capture readers' attention both in print and as an interactive online document. In addition, Adobe InDesign CS5 makes it easy to convert a print document to Flash Player (SWF) or Flash Professional (FLA) format without writing code, so you can focus on designing your layout.

When you gain the ability to easily create compelling online experiences from print documents using InDesign, you can potentially save money by not requiring additional software and reducing your printing, materials, and shipping costs as well as your carbon footprint.

You'll start by taking a look at the finished City Guide online document.

1 Open your Lesson03 folder on your desktop, open the folder Export SWF, and double-click the file City_Guide_Final.html to open it in your default web browser. This file includes a SWF file that plays back in the Flash Player plug-in in your web browser.

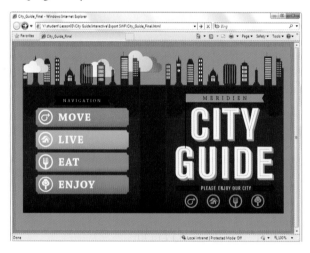

▶ **Tip:** When designing specifically for the web, consider using a horizontal page layout.

2 Click the Move button. Notice that this document includes animation in addition to interactivity.

3 In the bottom-right corner of the City_Guide_Final document, move the cursor over the Nav button. It expands to reveal navigational controls. Click the right arrow to see the next page, and explore the rest of the pages by clicking the right arrow again.

4 Click the Map button in the Nav panel. In the legend on the left side, click the Move, Eat, Live, and Enjoy buttons to see how they show and hide different groups of points of interest on the map.

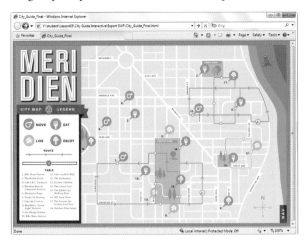

You can leave this web page open for reference as you work on this project during the lesson.

5 Open your Lesson03 folder on your desktop, and double-click the file City_Guide_Start.indd. If you see a message asking if you want to upgrade links, click Upgrade Links.

6 Choose File > Save As, and save the document to your Lesson03 folder as **City_Guide.indd**.

7 Go from spread to spread to explore the document.

Adding animation

The default workspace in InDesign CS5 hides the animation panels, but choosing a different workspace quickly brings them to the forefront for your convenience. Animations you create in InDesign are preserved when you export to Flash Player or Flash Professional. In addition, InDesign CS5 comes with the same motion presets as Flash Professional CS5, and if you create motion presets in Flash Professional CS5, InDesign CS5 can use them. This means that animations you create in InDesign don't exist in isolation—you're building a foundation that you can optionally enhance using Flash Professional CS5.

1   In the Application bar, choose Interactive from the workspaces menu. This rearranges the panels to make the animation and interactivity controls the most prominent along the right side of the workspace.

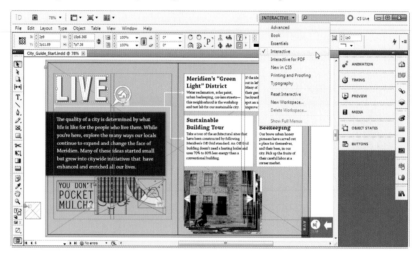

2   Go to page 6, and with the Selection tool, select the LIVE headline at the upper-left corner of the page.

3   In the Animation panel, choose Fly in from Top from the Preset menu. This applies an Adobe Flash motion preset to the selected object. In the Animation panel, the butterfly graphic previews the effect for you.

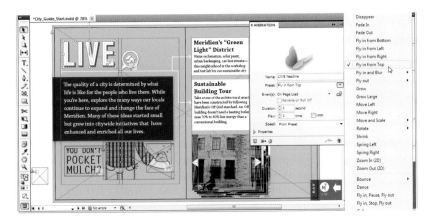

4 Click the Preview Spread button at the bottom-left corner of the Animation panel. This opens the Preview panel, where you can evaluate the current state of the animation.

The LIVE headline moved last because it was the last animation that was created. However, you want it to be the first object to animate, so you'll change the animation order using the Timing panel.

The Preview panel is fully interactive, so if you want to test buttons without exporting the project, the Preview panel is the place to do it. It's a good idea to enlarge the Preview panel to make it easier to click buttons and links.

Comparing buttons and hyperlinks

You can use buttons and hyperlinks to build navigation controls in InDesign. While at first glance it might seem that there's overlap between what buttons and hyperlinks can do, to choose between them, you need to know a few key differences in how they work.

Buttons are generally graphic in nature, such as a picture or drawn object that you set up as a button. A button works much like a graphics frame; for example, you can replace the contents of a button. Buttons can also have multiple states. Options for buttons are in the Buttons panel (Window > Interactive > Buttons). You're more likely to use buttons in graphically engaging multimedia projects, where appearance and compelling interactivity is important.

Hyperlinks are generally text-based and can be generated from text. For example, InDesign can create a live URL hyperlink from URL text you've selected. Hyperlinks have fewer display and rollover options than buttons, and can handle only a couple of basic states. Hyperlink options are in the Hyperlinks panel (Window > Interactive > Hyperlinks). You're more likely to use hyperlinks in a text-heavy reference document, where the hyperlinks may be automatically generated and also automatically preserved when you export the file to PDF.

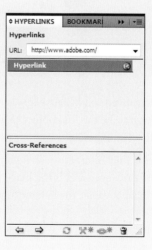

5 In the Timing panel, drag LIVE Headline from the bottom of the list to the top.

6 In the Timing panel, select Fly 1, Fly 2, and Fly 3, click the Play Together button, and preview the spread again. This is an easy way to play multiple animations simultaneously.

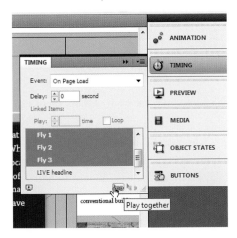

You've successfully added and edited an animation in InDesign. Next you'll add buttons with multiple states that can respond to mouse rollovers.

Adding interactive elements

When you publish a brochure (or a newsletter, or flyer—you name it) for onscreen viewing rather than for print, you typically need to add interactive content so that readers can navigate the document online.

Creating multi-state objects

With InDesign CS5 you can easily create multi-state objects, which are commonly used to improve interaction feedback for buttons. You can also use multi-state objects to augment the media that was in your print layout as in the following steps, where the space that contained one image in the print layout can contain multiple images in the online layout.

1   Close any open panels, and open the Layers panel (press F7).

2   In the Layers panel, click the selection box for the Multi-State Objects layer to select all of the objects on that layer, which are pictures.

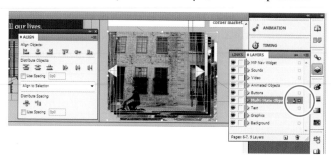

Leave the objects selected for the rest of the steps; you'll use each of these pictures as a different object state.

▶ **Tip:** InDesign shows and hides options on the Control panel depending on the width of the monitor. If you want to see an option that there isn't room to show in the Control panel, you can make room by hiding options. Click the panel menu at the right edge of the Control panel and choose Customize.

3   In the Control panel, click the Align Top Edges button, and then click the Align Left Edges button. If you don't see these buttons in the Control panel, your monitor may not be wide enough to display them; in that case choose Window > Object & Layout > Align, and click the same buttons in the Align panel.

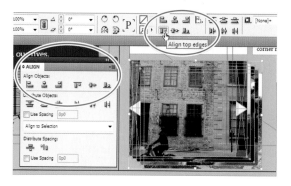

The Align buttons are a quick and easy way to make sure all states are lined up.

Online publishing with the EPUB format

The rise of eBook readers brought about the need for a standard format optimized for onscreen reading. A format performing this role is EPUB, a digital version of a conventional printed book. The EPUB format is a free, open eBook standard. EPUB files can be read on a diverse range of eBook readers—from handheld devices (like the Sony Reader and Barnes & Noble nook) to desktop reading applications (like Adobe Digital Editions) and smartphone reading applications (like Stanza on the iPhone and iPad).

The EPUB format is an XML-based format designed to enable text to reflow according to the capabilities of various eBook readers, which means that you can resize the text, change the font, or view an eBook on different screen sizes, and the text will reflow to fill the available view area. This makes the EPUB format the best choice for eBooks that are read on small, handheld reading devices. In contrast, PDF preserves the original layout of a document, giving you complete control over page design and presentation. PDF is the optimal choice for eBooks that have a complex design or will only be read on regular-sized computer screens.

Because EPUB is XML-based, the format can be converted into other proprietary formats such as the MOBI format, which is compatible with the Amazon Kindle. For detailed instructions on converting an EPUB file into the MOBI format, see the technical paper "From Adobe InDesign to the Kindle Store" at www.adobe.com/products/indesign/pdfs/indesigntokindle_wp_ue.pdf.

The EPUB format does not define page structure, so all the content flows together in one continuous linear stream. This can present a problem for publications that have an elaborate design. If your layout is quite simple, you probably won't notice much of a difference between it and its eBook equivalent. Because the EPUB format is based on XML, which is similar to the CSS web standard, the more a publication is formatted similarly to a CSS layout the higher the chance that the document will translate well to EPUB.

Some publications may be too design-intensive to be properly presented as an EPUB file. In such cases, PDF is a more suitable format for online viewing.

InDesign CS5 can export directly to the EPUB format when you choose File > Export for > EPUB. In the Digital Editions Export Options dialog box, you can specify how formatting in the InDesign file will be translated to EPUB format.

To preview your EPUB documents, use Adobe Digital Editions software, a free download from adobe.com.

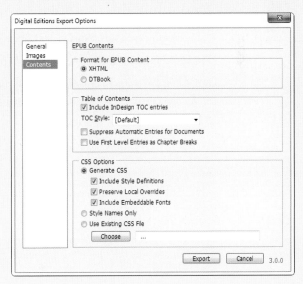

4   Click the Properties triangle at the bottom of the Animation panel to reveal more options, and choose Fade In from the Opacity menu.

5   In the Object States panel, click the Convert Selection to Multi-State Object button. InDesign uses the selected objects to create a single object with multiple states that now appear in the Object States panel.

6   Now try it out. Click the various states in the Object States panel to see how the multi-state object changes on the layout.

7   In the Object States panel, select State 1. You'll leave the object in this state.

8   Choose Edit > Deselect All so that no objects are selected on the layout.

You've created a single object with multiple states; each picture is now a state that can be displayed. To let a reader flip through the pictures, you'll add buttons next.

Creating buttons from objects

Each photo in the multi-state object includes a pair of triangle graphics that are intended to be used as buttons. At this point they're just graphics, but you'll now make them function as buttons.

1 With the Selection tool, select the tall, narrow object containing the triangle at the left edge of the multi-state object.

2 In the Buttons panel, click the Actions + button (add an action), and choose Go to Previous State.

3 Select the object containing the triangle on the right side of the multi-state object and use the Buttons panel to add the Go to Next State action, just as you did in steps 1 and 2.

4   Drag the Preview panel tab to the left to separate it from the other panels, and enlarge the panel so that the buttons you just created are easier to see.

5   Click the Preview Spread button at the bottom-left corner of the Preview panel. After the initial animation plays, click the left and right buttons you just set up to test how well the buttons change the states of the multi-state object.

6   When you're done testing the buttons, drag the Preview panel tab back to the stack of other interactive panels to move it out of the way. Or you can click Interactive in the Application bar and choose Reset Interactive to restore the original arrangement of the Interactive workspace.

Adding a sound to a button

Now you'll make a button on another spread play a sound.

1   Go to page 12. If necessary, choose View > Fit Spread in Window to see the entire map.

You need to add a sound to a button for an establishment called The Grease Cart. There are many buttons on the map. While you could locate the correct button by using the legend, the designer of this file intelligently organized the objects using the Layers panel so the button would be easier to select as a layer.

2   In the Layers panel, expand the Buttons layer and click the selection box for the object Grease_Cart_btn to select it.

3   In the Buttons panel, click the Actions + button (add an action), choose Go
    to State, and then choose Location_PopUps_MSO from the Object menu.

4   In the Buttons panel, choose Grease_Cart from the State menu, click the
    Actions + button, and choose Sound. Notice that this adds Sound to the list
    of actions in the Buttons menu, meaning that when this button is released,
    InDesign will go to the specified state and play a sound. You still need to specify
    which sound to play, so you'll do that next.

5   In the Buttons panel, choose mapClick.mp3 from the Sound menu.

6   Click the Preview Spread button at the bottom-left corner of the Buttons panel,
    and enlarge the Preview panel as needed.

7   In the Preview panel, click the Eat button to display just the places where you
    can eat in the city of Meridien, and then click the fork icon in the middle, next
    to the legend number 14. This is the button you just set up.

Clicking the fork icon should display the state that appears as a pop-up window describing The Grease Cart (the state called Location_PopUps_MSO that you applied in step 3), and if you can hear your computer audio you should hear a click sound.

8   When you're done testing your work, close the Preview panel and the other panels you were using, or reset the Interactive workspace.

9   Save the InDesign document.

Next you'll add a video clip to the InDesign document, but there are a couple of things you need to do first. You'll add a text overlay to the video using the video editing features in Photoshop, and then you'll convert it to Flash video so that it can be delivered online as part of a Flash project.

Editing video in Photoshop

● **Note:** To work with multimedia in Adobe Creative Suite, such as playing back and editing video, your system must be running Apple QuickTime 7.6.2 or later. QuickTime is a free download from www.apple.com/quicktime/download.

When you import video into Photoshop Extended, the image frames are placed in a video layer. You can add layers above that video layer to apply image adjustments or to overlay text and graphics, and you can use the Animation (Timeline) panel to adjust how video layers play back.

1   Switch to Photoshop Extended CS5. Choose File > Open. In the Open dialog box, navigate to the Lesson03 folder. Select the file cycling_432x235_start.mov, and click Open.

2   Choose Window > Workspace > Motion. Notice the Animation (Timeline) panel across the bottom of the workspace. Drag the current-time indicator to navigate through the individual image frames of the movie, and then leave it at the beginning of the Timeline.

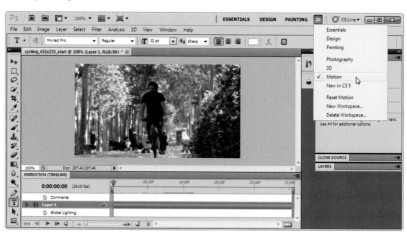

3   With the Type tool, click near the bottom-left corner of the video to create a new point text object, and type the text **Coming soon**.

4   With an insertion point blinking in the text, press Ctrl/Command-A to select all of the text.

5   In the Options bar, choose Chaparral Pro from the first (font) menu, choose Bold from the second (style) menu to match the type in the InDesign layout, and in the third menu enter a font size of **32**. The text should extend about halfway across the video frame if it's left-aligned; if it isn't, click the Left Align Text button in the middle of the Options bar.

6   With the text still selected, click the color swatch in the Options bar, click white in the color picker, and click OK.

7   Choose Layer > Layer Style > Drop Shadow, and when the Layer Style dialog box appears, click OK to accept the default settings. Adding a drop shadow helps make the text more legible against a changing background.

▶ **Tip:** The Drop Shadow command is also available by clicking the effects (fx) menu at the bottom of the Layers panel; you may find this to be faster than choosing the command on the menu bar.

8   Drag the current-time indicator through the movie to see how the type looks.

9   In the Animation (Timeline) panel, drag the right end of the green bar for the Coming Soon layer to the left until it reaches the five-second mark (05:00f). This displays the Coming Soon layer for five seconds, and then stops displaying it.

10 Choose File > Export > Render Video. Click Select Folder and navigate to your Lesson03 folder. Name the file **cycling_comingsoon.mov**, leave the rest of the options at their default settings, and click Render. Rendering may take some time, depending on your computer's performance.

11 When video rendering is complete, close Photoshop and save changes.

The video content is ready, but it needs to be converted to Flash video since the InDesign document you'll add it to will be exported to Flash. Because Flash video formats are not options in the Render Video dialog box, the video is still in QuickTime MOV format. Fortunately, converting to Flash video is quick and easy with Adobe Media Encoder.

Converting to Flash video

Adobe Media Encoder, included with Design Premium, can convert video files into common formats suitable for devices ranging from DVD players to websites to mobile phones to portable media players and standard- and high-definition TV sets. Adobe Media Encoder includes presets that greatly simplify the many output settings available for video formats. All you'll have to do is drag the video into Adobe Media Encoder, pick the right preset, and name the file.

1 Start Adobe Media Encoder CS5.

2 In your Lesson03 folder, drag the movie cycling_comingsoon.mov (the one you rendered from Photoshop) and drop it into the dark gray render queue list in the Adobe Media Encoder window.

3 Click the triangle under the Preset menu and choose F4V – Match Source Attributes (High Quality).

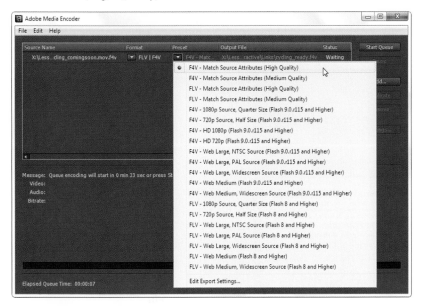

F4V is the latest and most capable version of the Flash video format.

4 Click the path in the Output File column, make sure the destination is set to your Lesson03 folder, and change the name of the file to **cycling_ready**.

The final filename will be cycling_ready.f4v because Adobe Media Encoder will automatically apply the correct filename extension for the file format specified in the preset you chose.

5 Click Start Queue.

If you don't click Start Queue, the queue will start on its own in two minutes. When needed, you can queue up several video clips and let Adobe Media Encoder render them in the background while you do something else.

6 When rendering is complete, exit Adobe Media Encoder.

Adding video to an InDesign document

▶ **Tip:** New in InDesign CS5 is the ability to place Flash video (FLV or F4V), the most common video format on the web. You can drag Flash video directly into an InDesign layout, simplifying the conversion of print documents into compelling online content.

You've already begun adding multimedia to the online document by adding a sound to a button; now add a video clip to the document.

1 Go to page 11. In the upper-right corner of the spread is an empty frame. For the print version it contained a photo, but for online viewing it's intended to contain a video, which you will now place.

2 Magnify the view to zoom in on the empty frame, and in the Media panel click the Place A Video Or Audio File button at the bottom-right corner of the panel.

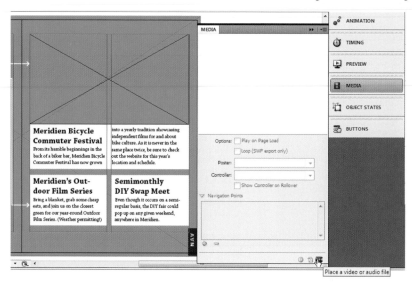

● **Note:** You must have Acrobat 6.*x* or later to play MPEG and SWF movies in a PDF file—or Acrobat 5.0 or later to play QuickTime and AVI movies.

3 In the Place Media dialog box, navigate to your Lesson03 folder, and double-click the movie cycling_ready.mov that you converted using Adobe Media Encoder. The mouse cursor becomes a place cursor loaded with the movie file.

4 Click the loaded place cursor in the placeholder frame.

5 In the Media panel, click the Play button to watch the video.

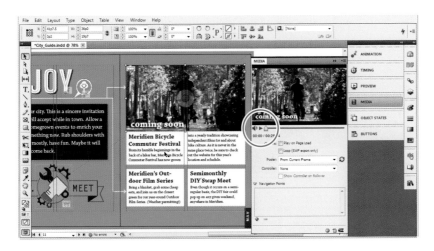

By default, the InDesign document uses the first frame of the video as the poster frame—the frame shown on the layout. Now you'll find a more dynamic frame to use as the poster frame.

6   In the Media panel, drag the slider until you find a frame that you think is more compelling as a poster frame, such as a frame just before the 12-second mark. Then click the reload button (⟳) to the right of the Poster menu to apply the frame you're viewing to the layout as the poster frame.

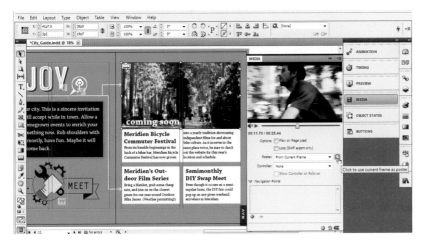

7 In the Media panel, choose SkinOverAllNoCaption from the Controller menu, and select the Show Controller on Rollover check box.

8 In the Preview panel, click the Preview Spread button at the bottom-left corner of the pane. This preview might take a little longer to generate since a movie is involved. Make sure the poster frame is the one you selected, and move the mouse over the movie to test whether the controller appears as you set it in step 7.

Exporting in SWF (Shockwave Flash) format

▶ **Tip:** Before you export an InDesign document to an online format such as SWF, choose Edit > Transparency Blend Space and make sure it's set to Document RGB. Documents produced for print are often built using a CMYK color model and blend space.

When you've finished adding animation and interactivity to your print document, you can export directly to SWF (Shockwave Flash) format for easy deployment on a website.

1 Choose File > Export.

2 In the Export dialog box, navigate to the Lesson03 folder, choose Flash Player (SWF) from the Save As Type/Format menu, name the file **City_Guide_Screen.swf**, and then click Save.

3 In the Export SWF dialog box that appears, you can leave the default settings except for one: Deselect the Include Interactive Page Curl checkbox. Then click OK.

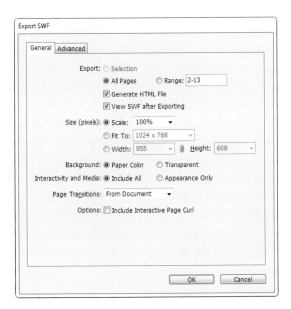

InDesign exports the SWF file and opens the accompanying HTML file in your default web browser. It should look much like the sample you viewed at the beginning of this lesson.

4 When you're done, close the web page and return to InDesign.

Tip: You can upload the files to your web server and have your client preview the page design in a standard web browser.

Exporting to Flash Professional

You can go beyond the interactivity tools in InDesign by enhancing your project in Flash Professional CS5. The workflow between InDesign and Flash Professional CS5 is integrated so that you can design an interactive experience using the design tools in InDesign, and then export the project to Flash Professional CS5 so that a web developer can enhance the project using the full power of Flash Professional CS5 without having to re-create the design. Flash Professional CS5 preserves key design attributes such as InDesign layers, typographic quality, and text threading between frames.

1. In InDesign, choose File > Export.

2. In the Export dialog box, navigate to the Lesson03 folder, choose Flash Professional CS5 (FLA) from the Save As Type/Format menu, name the file **City_Guide_fp.fla**, and then click Save. The Export Flash CS5 Professional (FLA) dialog box appears. Leave the options at their default settings, and then click OK to complete the export.

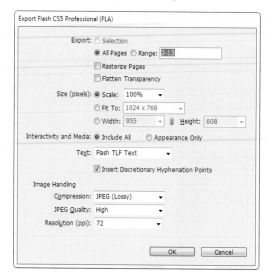

3. In your Lesson03 folder, double-click the file City_Guide_fp.fla. It opens in Flash Professional.

4. In Flash Professional, press the period key (.) to step forward one frame. Press it again to step through the five Timeline frames that represent the five pages that were in the InDesign document. Press the comma key (,) to step back a frame.

5. Navigate to frame 2 and double-click one of the white text frames. This lets you edit frame 2.

The conversion of InDesign documents to Flash Professional is greatly improved in Flash Professional CS5. You can see some of the conversion improvements in this frame. All of the layers from InDesign have been preserved. Also, when a text frame is selected, you can see that the threading between text frames has been preserved. The text inside the frames displays at a high level of typographic quality, because Flash Professional CS5 uses a new text engine called TLF that preserves the level of typography you've traditionally appreciated in InDesign.

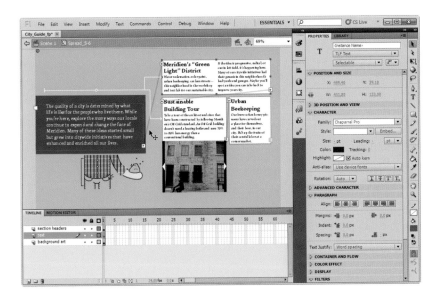

6 When you're done, close Flash Professional and return to InDesign.

You learned about starting from an InDesign document designed for both print and online output, adding hyperlinks and interactive elements, adjusting movies in Photoshop, and exporting for Flash Player and Flash Professional. For more in-depth coverage of all these subjects, refer to Help in each of the applications and the other books in the Classroom in a Book series.

Review questions

1 When would you want to export an InDesign document to Flash Player (SWF) format, and when would you want to export to the Flash Professional (FLA) format?

2 In InDesign, which panel controls the order in which objects animate?

3 How do you test interactions and animations in InDesign?

4 What is a poster frame, and how do you set it?

5 What are some of the differences between exporting as a PDF document and exporting as an EPUB document?

Review answers

1 Export to Flash Player when you want to create an interactive experience that's ready to deploy online. Export to Flash Professional when you want to enhance the project further using the full toolset of Flash Professional; for example, to hand off to a Flash developer who can write code to produce a more immersive and compelling version of your project than you can achieve with InDesign alone.

2 The Timing panel controls the order in which objects animate in InDesign.

3 Test interactions and animations using the Preview panel.

4 A poster frame is the frame that represents a video in an InDesign layout. By default the poster frame is the first frame of a video, but you can change that in the Poster menu in the Media panel.

5 A PDF document preserves the original page layout so that the designer has complete control over the presentation; for example, the reader can't change the way type looks. In an EPUB document, text can reflow to fit the size of a display, and the reader can typically adjust type attributes such as font and size to improve readability on their device.

4 CREATING INTERACTIVE FLASH CONTENT

Lesson Overview

In this lesson, you'll learn the following:

- Creating a Flash Catalyst document
- Editing pages and states
- Creating interactivity
- Animating transitions
- Roundtrip editing with Adobe Illustrator
- Adding video
- Publishing to SWF format

 This lesson will take about two hours to complete.

Start with compelling graphics designed using Adobe Illustrator. Add interactivity, navigation buttons, and video, and animate the graphics. Export the project as a fully functional Adobe AIR rich-media application, ready to be deployed online.

About Adobe Flash Catalyst

New from Adobe, Flash Catalyst helps designers easily build rich, interactive content. It combines an intuitive user interface with a toolset that will feel familiar—similar to Photoshop, Illustrator, and Fireworks—with the expressiveness, consistency, and reach of Adobe Flash technology. The result: a feature-rich interaction design tool you can successfully use to publish SWF files without writing code.

As you'd expect from a professional Adobe design tool, you always have complete control over the appearance of your artwork, and you can publish your interactive content as a SWF file that displays with Adobe Flash Player 10 for wide browser compatibility on the web.

If you want a developer to enhance an interactive project you've built with Flash Catalyst, you don't have to do anything. Flash Catalyst output is developer-friendly, writing code for you in the background while you focus on designing expressive, interactive content. Using the open-source Adobe Flex framework as its underlying structure, Flash Catalyst helps ensure that when you have to hand more complex projects off to a developer, everything is already in place, ready to go.

A typical workflow

To create an interactive document in Flash Catalyst, you typically perform the following steps:

1 Plan how the user should interact with your document, and also plan transitions between states or pages.

2 Design the document in Adobe Illustrator or Adobe Photoshop, using layers to structure the content in a way that supports the buttons, states, and other interactivity you'll apply in Flash Catalyst.

3 Import the design and any multimedia assets into your Flash Catalyst document.

4 Add interactivity and transitions.

5 Test and publish your document.

Viewing the sample document

You will start by opening a Flash document provided in the Lesson04 folder. It's an interactive banner intended to work within a larger website design.

1   In Windows Explorer/the Finder, navigate to your Lesson04 folder. In the Banner_finished folder, open the InteractiveBanner_SWF folder. Double-click the file Main.html.

2   In your web browser, explore the Flash document. Move the mouse over the five buttons at the top of the banner, and notice how the buttons highlight and make a sound as the cursor passes over them. At the bottom-left corner is an article link (it doesn't actually go to the web in this demonstration), and at the middle of the bottom is a scrollable text field.

3   Move the cursor to the right edge to highlight the navigation arrow, and click it to see the second panel. Then click button 4 at the top of the banner to go to the fourth panel.

4   The fourth panel contains a movie. Click the Play button in the middle of the movie to watch it. Feel free to explore the other panels.

Comparing Flash Catalyst and Flash Professional

Flash Catalyst complements Flash Professional by letting designers easily create immersive online experiences by transforming visually compelling artwork they create using tools such as Adobe Illustrator and Adobe Photoshop. Typical Flash Catalyst projects focus on user interface design, rich Internet applications, micro-sites, prototypes, and widgets. Its structured approach to interaction design greatly simplifies the creation of rich media by designers. Use Flash Catalyst when you want to start with highly designed content and end with a finished project, or a project that you can hand off to a web developer to enhance using Flex Builder, all without writing a single line of code.

In contrast, Flash Professional is a more developer-oriented tool focused on creating immersive experiences that can include video content. Typical Flash Professional projects focus on rich content, highly interactive video content, advertising, and games. Its free-form, fully timeline-driven approach, and advanced vector anima-tion provides a much wider range of possibilities for user interaction than is avail-able from Flash Catalyst. While Flash Catalyst can create output for Flash Player and Adobe AIR, Flash Professional also supports mobile devices through Flash Lite and iPhone export capability. The wider scope of potential offered by Flash Professional often requires at least some coding and a steeper learning curve than Flash Catalyst.

5 You can keep this document open as reference as you go through this lesson. If you don't want to leave it open right now, close the web browser window or tab, or exit the web browser.

Next you'll open the Flash Catalyst document that was used to create the interac-tive Flash document.

6 Start Adobe Flash Catalyst.

7 Click the Open button in the Welcome screen, or choose File > Open Project.

8 In the Open Project dialog box, navigate to your Lesson04 folder. In the Banner_finished folder, open the InteractiveBanner_FC folder. Double-click the file InteractiveBanner_finished.fxp.

Across the top of the window you can see the five pages of the banner. The top of the workspace contains view controls, and many of the tools you'll use are available along the right side of the workspace, starting with the tools at the top and then a column of panels. The Timelines and Design-Time Data panels are minimized at the bottom of the workspace.

Creating a Flash Catalyst document

You'll create a new Flash Catalyst document. This will be the foundation for the design and interactivity that you'll add later.

1   In the Flash Catalyst welcome screen, click Adobe Flash Catalyst Project. If you don't see the welcome screen, choose Welcome.

2   Name the project **Banner**. For the width enter **955**, for the height enter **310,** and then click OK. The new blank document appears, and the document that was previously open is closed.

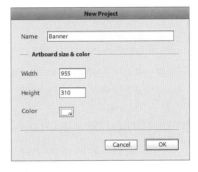

3   To see the entire content of the artboard in the document window, choose View > Fit Artboard In Window.

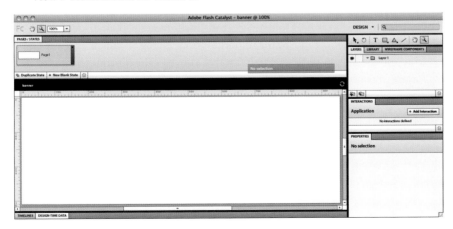

4 At the top of the workspace, in the application bar to the left of the search field, click the Design menu and choose Code.

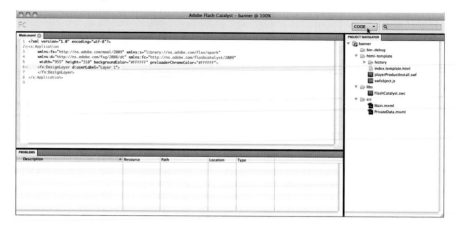

Design and Code are the two document workspaces in Flash Catalyst. As you work, Flash Catalyst creates code in the background so that a web developer can build upon your work using Flash Builder. You can see that Flash Catalyst has already generated code for the new blank document. You can't edit the code in Flash Catalyst; you'll be working in Design workspace during this lesson.

5 Switch from Code workspace back to Design workspace.

6 Choose File > Save As, and save the document under the name **Banner** in your Lesson04 folder.

Importing a design from Adobe Illustrator

You can import Adobe Illustrator or Adobe Photoshop graphics directly onto the artboard, preserving all layers and the image composition. In this exercise you'll import the design for the banner created in Adobe Illustrator.

1 Choose File > Import > Adobe Illustrator File (.ai).

2 Navigate to your Lesson04 folder. Select the file InteractiveBanner_art.ai, and click Open. When the Illustrator Import Options dialog box appears, click OK to accept the default settings. Flash Catalyst converts the Illustrator document for use in Flash Catalyst. If the Import Issues dialog box appears, click OK.

Designing Layers for Flash Catalyst

When you prepare graphics in Adobe Illustrator or Adobe Photoshop as the basis for a Flash Catalyst project, be sure to plan ahead and organize your Illustrator and Photoshop documents into layers and layer groups that anticipate the structure of the interactive media you'll create in Flash Catalyst.

For example, in the Illustrator document that's used as the foundation for the Flash Catalyst project in this chapter, a top-level Panels layer contains sublayers that correspond to each of the banner's five panels. Each panel's sublayer contains the objects belonging to that panel.

At points during the lesson, multiple objects are converted into a Flash Catalyst component. Because the layer hierarchy from Illustrator already corresponds to the hierarchy of the components that will be created in Flash Catalyst, it takes only one click in the Layers panel to select all the objects needed for a specific component.

3   The Illustrator artwork you just imported may be selected; if it is, choose Edit > Deselect All. You may also want to choose View > Fit Artboard In Window.

Now you'll add interactivity and navigation to the Illustrator graphics you imported.

Creating a scroll bar

Now you'll turn a graphic of a scroll bar into an actual, working scroll bar. This is easy because Flash Catalyst already knows about the most common interactive controls. All you have to do is assign specific graphics to become those controls.

1 Choose View > Magnification > 200% and adjust the view so that you can see the scroll bar graphic to the right of the paragraph in the center of the banner.

2 With the Selection tool, Shift-click to select both the scroll bar thumb and its track.

As soon as you select objects, a floating Heads Up Display (HUD) appears, presenting context-sensitive options for the selected object. You'll use the HUD to quickly create a working scroll bar from the selected graphics. If the HUD is in the way, you can drag it to another position.

3 With the two objects selected, choose Vertical Scrollbar from the Convert Artwork to Component menu. The HUD changes to lead you through the next step, indicating which graphics correspond to the parts of a working scroll bar.

4 In the HUD, click Edit Parts.

5 Select the larger object that will become the scroll bar track, and in the HUD select "Track (required)" from the Convert to Vertical Scrollbar Part menu.

6 Select the smaller object that will become the scroll bar thumb control, and in the HUD select "Thumb (required)" from the Convert to Vertical Scrollbar Part menu.

You'll see the word "Required" in the menu when Flash Catalyst knows that a control can't function without that part. You're done setting up the scroll bar, because you've already assigned objects to both required parts—the scroll bar track and the thumb control.

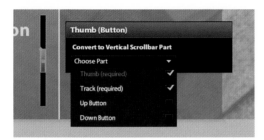

7 Choose File > Run Project. Flash Catalyst builds a temporary version of the project and opens it in your default web browser.

8 In your web browser, test that the scroll bar is working properly.

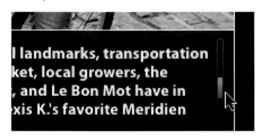

Creating a scrolling text panel

Now that your scroll bar works, you can bind it to a text panel to make the text scrollable when it's too big for the panel. You'll do this the same way you just created a scroll bar out of two objects—by converting the scroll bar and a text panel into a component. This associates the scroll bar with the text panel so that Flash Catalyst knows which panel is controlled by that particular scroll bar.

1 Switch back to Flash Catalyst. Just above the artboard is a *crumb trail* that works like a folder path, telling you what you're editing in the document. Right now it reads Banner/VerticalScrollbar1. It isn't just an indicator; it also lets you control which level of the document you're editing. Click the word Banner to exit scroll bar editing mode.

2 Select the scroll bar and the text panel next to it.

3 With the two objects selected, choose Scroll Panel from the Convert Artwork to Component menu. The HUD changes to lead you through editing the parts of the scroll panel.

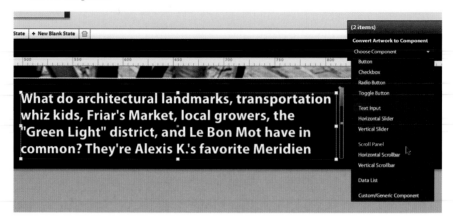

4 In the HUD, click Edit Parts. Because the scroll bar already exists in the selection, the only required part to assign is the scrolling content, so select the text panel and then choose Scrolling Content (required) from the Choose Part menu.

5 Choose File > Run Project, and test the scrolling panel in your web browser.

Now you'll group the objects in the lower part of the banner to make it easier to work with as a unit later, when you apply transitions. There are many objects involved, but because they're already arranged within the same layer, you can select all of them at once using the Layers panel.

6 In Flash Catalyst, click Banner in the crumb trail. In the Layers panel, click the triangle next to the Panels layer to expand it; expand the Feature panel sublayer and click the Feature panel sublayer to select it and all of the objects inside it.

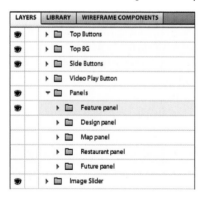

7 With the objects still selected, choose Custom/Generic Component from the Convert Artwork to Component menu.

When you combine objects into a component, Flash Catalyst can optimize that component more easily than if it was still multiple objects. Now you're ready to provide visual feedback and context that will reinforce the interactivity you'll add.

Editing pages and states

With the Pages/States panel in Flash Catalyst, you can define how your design responds to viewer interactions. With Pages, different parts of your design can respond to viewer interaction, such as a button changing another part of your design. With States, you can control how individual components respond, such as the button itself.

Now you'll create the buttons that allow the user to go from one page to the next.

1 In the Layers panel, expand the Top Buttons layer. If necessary, zoom out so that you can see the five buttons at the top of the banner.

2 Click the Button1 sublayer to select all the objects that make up Button1.

3 In the HUD, choose Button from the Convert Artwork to Component menu.

4 Double-click button 1 on the artboard. Notice in the crumb trail that you are currently editing only the button, and the Pages/States panel now displays the different states of that button.

5 In the Pages/States panel, click the Over state.

6 In the Layers panel, expand the Button1 layer and turn off the Up layer.

● **Note:** As you work with objects in this lesson, you may see the same object referred to in more than one way. For example, you might see references to button 1 and Button1. When you see a reference such as button 1, look for a button on the artboard labeled 1. When you see a capitalized name with no space (such as Button1), that's an object name that you'll find in a panel such as Layers or Library.

7 Click the Down state, and in the Layers panel turn off the Up and Over layers.

8 Click the Disabled state, and in the Layers panel turn off the Up and Over layers.

The orange Down layer will now be visible as long as the mouse button is down over a button, and also when you're already on the target page for a button.

You have now created all the different states for that button when the user mouses over and clicks on the button.

9   In the Pages/States panel, click each of the states to preview how the button looks during viewer interactions.

Setting up a label

When your design uses multiple copies of an object, you can represent them with multiple instances of a single component. To differentiate them during interactions, you can convert the object's text into a label that you change for each instance of the component. Using instances and labels instead of making whole copies of objects makes the project more efficient and easier to store and optimize. In this project, the buttons are identical except for the number, so you'll turn the numbers into labels.

1   With the Button1 sublayer selected in the Layers panel, click the Up state in the Pages/States panel; then in the Layers panel, expand the Button sublayer and click the layer named **label** that contains a 1.

2   In the HUD, choose Label from the Convert to Button Part menu.

Note that although the layer is already named Label, that was just a name assigned in Illustrator to remind you to convert the text into a label in Flash Catalyst.

3   In the crumb trail, click Banner to exit button editing mode.

4   Click the Library tab to open the Library panel, expand the Components section if necessary, and then select Button1 in the Components section. Drag Button1 from the Library panel over button 2 on the artboard. Don't be concerned that Button1 doesn't match the square shape of button 2 on the artboard; align the top-left corner with the top-left corner of the existing square button.

When you created a working Button1 component earlier, it was added to the Library panel. In this step you're adding another instance of the same button so that you don't have to create it again. Now you'll customize the label of the new button 2.

5   With the button selected (not the text), in the Properties panel expand the Common properties if necessary, and for Label enter **2**. The text is now short enough to fit inside the button because you edited it down to the number 2.

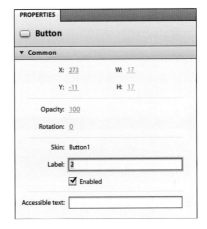

6   On the artboard, select the first button in the row of buttons you're working with. This also selects it (Button 2) in the Layers panel. Double-click the name of the selected button and change its name to Button 1. You're replacing the button graphics imported from Illustrator with interactive button components you've just built in Flash Catalyst. In the same way, edit the second button so its layer name is Button 2.

7   In the Layers panel, delete the Button2 sublayer (the one that looks like a folder, not the new button component you just added and renamed). You don't need it anymore, because you just replaced it with a working button.

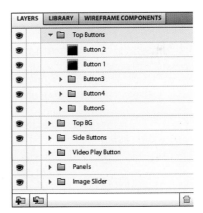

In an actual project, you'd continue this process to replace the other three top buttons. For this lesson, you'll move on to creating a transition between pages 1 and 2 of the interactive banner.

Setting up pages and states for a transition

You can set up a transition that you can customize extensively by animating multiple objects. In this section you'll set up how the project experience changes during different states of interaction, and then in the next section you'll set up the events that animate them.

You may want to review the final project in your web browser to understand where each component of the project will move during this page transition.

1 In the Pages/States panel, click Page1.

2 In the Layers panel, turn off the FeaturepanelCustomComponent layer, and turn on the Design Panel layer. This sets the visibility of these layers when the viewer is on page 1.

3 Select the Design Panel sublayer in the Layers panel. With all the objects in that sublayer selected, create a custom component in the same way you did for the Feature panel in step 7 of Creating a Scrolling Text Panel, earlier in this lesson.

You may want to zoom out a level or two before the next step, so that there's a little space below the artboard.

4 With the DesignpanelCustomComponent layer selected, Shift-drag the component downward until it is off the artboard to set the initial position of the layer before a page transition starts.

5   Turn on the FeaturepanelCustomComponent layer and make sure the DesignpanelCustomComponent layer is still visible off the artboard.

6   In the Pages/States panel, click the Duplicate State button to create a new page called Page2. If the Timelines and Design-Time Data panels open at the bottom of the workspace and take up too much space on your screen, double-click the Timelines panel tab to minimize the panel group.

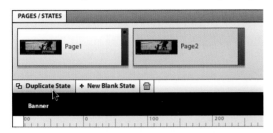

7   In the Layers panel, select the FeaturepanelCustomComponent layer, and Shift-drag the custom component downward until it is off the artboard; then hide it in the Layers panel.

8   Select the DesignpanelCustomComponent layer and Shift-drag it onto the artboard until it is positioned properly. In the Layers panel, make FeaturepanelCustomComponent visible again.

9   Still on Page2, select the Image Slider sublayer and use the HUD to turn it into a custom component.

10 With the ImageSliderCustomComponent layer selected, Shift-drag the component to the left until it is positioned properly between the two gray dark rectangles at the left and right sides of the page. This moves the image on Page2 into place to complete this page transition.

Setting up button navigation

After you've defined the different pages and states of interaction, you set up the buttons that will move the viewer between the pages and states.

1 In the Pages/States panel, click Page1, and then on the artboard select button 1.

2 In the Interactions panel, click Add Interaction.

3 Choose On Click from the first menu.

4 Choose Play Transition to State from the second menu.

5 Choose Page1 from the Choose State menu, and click OK.

6   Still on the Page1 state, select button 2 and repeat steps 2–5, except in step 5 choose page 2 as the target state.

7   In the Pages/States panel, click Page1, and then on the artboard select button 1.

8   In the Common section of the Properties panel, make sure the Enabled check box is not selected, because you don't want Button1 to do anything on Page1.

9   Click button 2, and in the Properties tab, make sure the Enabled check box is selected.

10   In the Pages/States panel, select Page2.

11   Click button 1, and in the Properties panel, make sure the Enabled check box is selected.

12   Click button 2, and in the Properties panel, make sure the Enabled check box is not selected.

13   Choose File > Run Project, and test your work by clicking the 1 and 2 buttons. Notice the transition you created between pages 1 and 2 and also how each button changes in appearance when you move the cursor over each of them.

Creating transitions

With the pages, states, and buttons all in place, you can now use the Timelines panel to control what happens over time during the transitions among pages and states.

1   Open the Timelines panel at the bottom-left corner of the workspace.

Notice that two state transitions already exist in the Timelines panel: Page1 to Page2 and Page2 to Page1. Also, note that all the layers that have been dragged onto and off the artboard have a layer in the Timelines panel that indicates the elements moved.

2 In the State Transitions section of the Timelines panel, make sure Page1 > Page2 is selected, and select the DesignpanelCustomComponent layer.

3 Position the cursor over the vertical bar that says Move and you will see a small handle appear.

4 Click the handle and drag the bar until it is at the 0.25 second mark, and then repeat for the FeaturepanelCustomComponent layer.

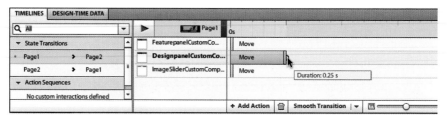

You want the Design panel (DesignpanelCustomComponent) to move onto the artboard after the 2 Wheels Good panel has moved off the artboard.

5 Click and drag the green bar for FeaturepanelCustomComponent movement so that it starts at the 0.25 second mark and ends at the 0.5 second mark.

6 For the ImageSliderCustomComponent layer, make the movement last for 0.5 seconds.

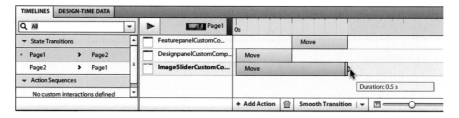

You can test the transitions within Adobe Flash Catalyst without running the project.

7 In the Timelines panel, click the Play button above the layer names.

Now, in much the same way, you'll create the transition that plays when the viewer navigates from Page2 back to Page1.

8 In the State Transitions section of the Timelines panel, make sure Page2 > Page1 is selected, and select the FeaturepanelCustomComponent layer.

9 With the FeaturepanelCustomComponent layer selected, click the handle and drag the bar until it is at the 0.25 second mark. Repeat for the DesignpanelCustomComponent layer.

10 You want the DesignpanelCustomComponent layer to move before the FeaturepanelCustomComponent, so drag the green bar representing the FeaturepanelCustomComponent animation so that it starts at the 0.25 second mark and ends at the 0.5 second mark.

11 For the ImageSliderCustomComponent layer, make the movement last for 0.5 seconds.

12 Click the Play button in the Timelines panel to test your animation.

13 Choose File > Run Project, and test the animation in your web browser.

Roundtrip editing with Adobe Illustrator

What happens if you need to make changes to the design after you've already applied interactivity in Flash Catalyst? Fortunately, you won't have to backtrack and lose work. Flash Catalyst integrates tightly with Adobe Illustrator so that after you import an Illustrator document into Flash Catalyst, you can open selected objects from the Flash Catalyst document in Adobe Illustrator, make changes, and return to Flash Catalyst without losing your interactivity.

1 In the Pages/States panel, click Page1.

2 In the Layers panel, click the Top BG sublayer to select the group at the top of the banner that includes the buttons.

3 With the group selected, choose Modify > Edit in Adobe Illustrator CS5 to open the banner objects in Illustrator. If the Enter Adobe ID dialog box appears, click Skip.

In Illustrator, the gray bar at the top of the document window tells you that you're editing graphics from Adobe Flash Catalyst.

4   Click the Layers panel icon to open the Layers panel, and click the target circle to the right of the Selected Content layer name to make sure the objects from Flash Catalyst are selected.

5   In the Control panel, click the Recolor Artwork button, and then in the Recolor Artwork, click the Edit tab.

6   Brighten the color by dragging the Brightness Adjuster slider to the right. The Brightness Adjuster is the first slider below the color wheel.

7   In the color wheel, drag the center circle anywhere on the color wheel.

8   Click the center of the color wheel and drag the second circle anywhere on the color wheel.

9   Click OK. If you don't want to make any more changes, click Done in the
    Editing from Adobe Flash Catalyst bar. When the FXG Options dialog box
    appears, click OK. The graphics in Flash Catalyst are updated.

Adding video

Video is an integral part of online media, and it's easy to add video or other multimedia to a Flash Catalyst project. You can easily control how the video plays and
whether playback controls are visible.

1   In Windows Explorer/the Finder, navigate to your Lesson04 folder. Inside the
    Banner_finished folder, open the InteractiveBanner_SWF folder. Double-click
    the file Main.html.

2 Click button 5, and then click the circular orange Play button. Watch how the video plays back.

For this part of the lesson, you'll use another version of the Flash Catalyst project in which all five panels are complete except for a video.

3 Switch to the desktop, and in your Lesson04 folder, double-click the file Video_start.fxp. (If you're asked to save changes for Banner.fxp, click Save.) Choose File > Save As, name the file **Video.fxp**, and click Save.

You'll now add the video to this Flash Catalyst project.

4 In the Pages/States panel, click Page5, and then choose View > Fit Artboard In Window so that you can see the entire artboard.

5 In the Layers panel, select the Feature Image layer. This is to make sure the video imports at the top level of the Layers panel, not inside a layer.

6 Choose File > Import > Video/Sound File. In your Lesson04 folder, select the cityscape.flv file and click Open. Notice that video controls are automatically displayed at the bottom of the video file.

7 With the video selected, in the Properties panel select None from the Video Controls menu because you won't use the built-in controls for playback.

8   Drag the Video Player layer until its top edge meets the top edge of the white
    area reserved for it in the design.

9   In the Layers panel, drag the Video Player layer downward until it's just below
    the Toggle Button layer.

10 In the Layers panel, select the Toggle Button layer. You'll set up this button so
    that it plays the movie.

11 In the Interactions panel, click Add Interaction. In the floating panel that
    appears, choose Play Video from the second menu, choose Video Player -
    cityscape1.flv from the Choose Video menu, and then click OK.

12 Choose File > Run Project to check your work.

Publishing to SWF for the web

Although Flash Catalyst can create code to be enhanced later by a web developer, for some projects you may find that you can reach all of your interaction design goals with Flash Catalyst alone. In these cases you can export directly to the SWF format for deployment on a web page.

You'll open the completed version of the project and export that to SWF.

1 Save your changes and close your Video.fxp project.

2 Choose File > Open Project, navigate to your Lesson04 folder, and inside that folder navigate to Banner_finished/InteractiveBanner_FC; select the file InteractiveBanner_finished.fxp and click OK.

3 In the menu bar, select File > Publish to SWF/AIR.

4 Navigate to your Lesson04 folder.

5 Leave the default settings as they are, and click Publish.

6 On the desktop, navigate to your Lesson04 folder. In that folder navigate to the InteractiveBanner_finished/run-local folder, and then double-click the Main.html file. Test the project.

You've successfully converted static Adobe Illustrator designs into dynamic, interactive online pieces using Flash Catalyst. You also used Adobe Illustrator to touch up the graphics using roundtrip editing. To use the finished project on your website, you would upload the entire Lesson04/InteractiveBanner_finished/InteractiveBanner_SWF folder, and then embed the Main.swf file on one of your web pages.

Review questions

1   Describe the typical workflow for creating a Flash Catalyst document.

2   Which applications can you use to create the graphics for a Flash Catalyst document, and why must you create them outside of Flash Catalyst?

3   What is the advantage of converting objects into a component?

4   In which panel do you define the duration of an animation?

5   Explain roundtrip editing between Flash Catalyst and Adobe Illustrator, and why it's advantageous.

Review answers

1   To create an interactive document in Flash, you typically perform the following steps:

   • Plan the animations and how the user should interact with your document.

   • Design the document in Adobe Illustrator or Adobe Photoshop.

   • Import the designed document and any other assets into your Flash Catalyst document.

   • Add interactivity and transitions.

   • Test and publish your document.

2   You create graphics for Flash Catalyst in Adobe Illustrator or Adobe Photoshop, so that you can use the powerful design tools in those programs to focus on graphic design. In Flash Catalyst, you focus on interaction design.

3   Combining objects into a component makes them easier to work with because they become a single unit, which makes it possible for Flash Catalyst to optimize the project further for online delivery.

4   You define the duration of an animation in the Timelines panel.

5   In roundtrip editing, you start by selecting objects in Flash Catalyst and opening them directly into Adobe Illustrator for editing. The advantages of the roundtrip workflow are that you don't have to take extra steps to export and import files between programs; and when you're done editing, the edited objects are returned to the Flash Catalyst document in place and ready to go without having to manually update or reimport files.

5 PROTOTYPING AND BUILDING A WEBSITE

Lesson Overview

In this lesson, you'll learn these skills and techniques:

- Prototyping a website in Fireworks
- Placing, scaling, and adjusting images
- Working with layers
- Adding a navigation bar
- Using master pages
- Adding dummy text and rollover behaviors
- Presenting the prototype
- Developing a website in Dreamweaver
- Setting up a page framework with CSS
- Incorporating pages from Fireworks
- Roundtrip editing between Fireworks and Dreamweaver

 This lesson will take about two hours to complete.

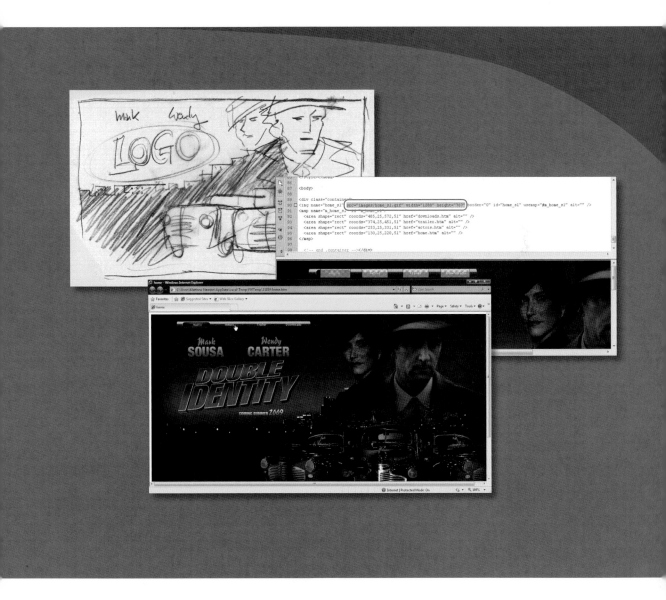

Learn how to use Fireworks to rapidly prototype a website design—complete with interactive links and rollover behaviors. Preview the pages in a standard web browser and get client approval before you start the website development in Dreamweaver. Incorporate the assets created in Fireworks and replace placeholder items.

● **Note:** Before you start working on this lesson, make sure that you've installed the Creative Suite 5 software on your computer and that you have correctly copied the Lessons folder from the CD in the back of this book onto your computer's hard disk (see "Copying the Classroom in a Book files" on page 2).

Planning for a website

Creating a website requires careful planning and preparation. Before spending a considerable amount of time coding the actual pages, you'll need to ensure that what you're developing is what your client expects. The desire of the client to see how the project will look when it's finished before approving the design can create a dilemma.

You need to present the client with a visual representation of the website design—ideally with fully functional rollover buttons and page links—without actually coding the pages in Dreamweaver.

The solution is to use Fireworks as a rapid prototyping tool. Fireworks enables you to quickly create a mock-up of a few pages of a website—including interactive elements—that can then be previewed in a standard web browser. Once the client approves the design, you can reuse the work you've done in Fireworks for the development of the website in Dreamweaver.

You can also use the same design prototype for more than just building a website.

A typical workflow

Designing a website from start to finish involves these basic steps:

1   Together with the client, define the scope of the project, including the objectives of the website, the target audience, schedule, and available resources.

2   Develop a design strategy and establish the look and feel of the web pages.

3   Create a prototype of the website in Fireworks.

4   Present the design to the client and refine it as necessary to obtain approval.

5   Assemble the required assets and create the website in Dreamweaver.

This lesson will focus on designing the website prototype in Fireworks and then incorporating that work into a Dreamweaver project.

The website you'll develop consists of a main page and three other pages, which are connected by hyperlinks as shown in the following illustration.

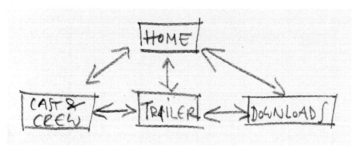

The design sketch for the home page shown in the following illustration was the result of a meeting with the client to establish the overall look and feel of the website.

Based on the design sketches, some images have been specially prepared, incorporating the common assets created in Lessons 1 and 2.

Previewing the assets in Bridge

To get a first impression of the images that will be used in this lesson, you can preview the files in your Lesson05 folder using Bridge.

1   Start Adobe Bridge CS5.

2   In Bridge, navigate to the Lesson05 folder on your hard disk. Within that folder, select the file CityBackground.psd. This image will serve as the background for the website pages.

3   In the Metadata panel, note the pixel dimensions for this image: 1280 x 787 pixels. This will be the page size—the size of the stage or canvas, if you prefer to using these terms—for the design in Fireworks.

4   Select the file Cars.psd. Only the car in the middle comes from a photo taken during the shooting of the film. The image of the car on the left was created from a 3D model as shown in Lesson 1. The car on the right is a flipped copy of the image on the left.

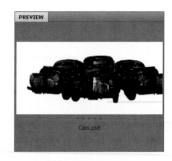

5   Select the file WendyAndMark.psd. The photos of the two main actors were placed on separate layers in the Photoshop file. The silhouettes were masked using the Quick Selection tool and the image background removed— a technique similar to that used for the brochure cover in Lesson 2.

6   Select the file LogoLockup.psd. The Double Identity logotype was designed in Illustrator and then placed in a Photoshop file. The other text was created in Photoshop by applying a gradient overlay to a type layer. For the purposes of this exercise, the type layers have been rasterized in case you don't have the appropriate fonts installed.

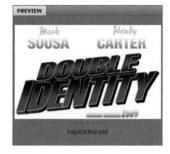

You won't use the rest of the images in the Lesson05 folder until later in this lesson.

Creating a prototype website in Fireworks

In the following exercises you'll work on two pages of a prototype website in Fireworks. In the process you'll place images, use layers to arrange and organize the page elements, create master pages for items that are shared across pages, add hyperlinks and rollover behaviors, and finally preview the design in a web browser.

Setting the stage

You'll begin by creating a new document in Fireworks.

1   Launch Adobe Fireworks CS5.

2   Click the Create New Fireworks Document (PNG) button in the Welcome screen, or choose File > New.

3   In the New Document dialog box, type **1280** in the Width text box and choose Pixels from the units menu beside it. Type **787** in the Height text box and choose Pixels from the units menu. Type **72** in the Resolution text box and choose Pixels/Inch from the resolution menu beside it. This is the default resolution for web pages. You can ignore the background color options under Canvas Color; for this prototype website, you will use an image as a background. Click OK.

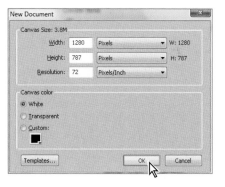

▶ **Tip:** You can adjust the setup options for the document at any time using the Property panel.

4   Choose File > Save As. In the Save As dialog box, navigate to your Lesson05 folder, select Fireworks PNG (*.png) from the Save As Type/Format menu, name the file Mockup.png, and then click Save.

Placing images

You can insert images into a Fireworks document in many different ways. You'll discover just a few of the options in the following exercises.

Using copy and paste

Copy an object or text in a variety of file formats from another application to the clipboard, and then use the Place command in Fireworks to insert the clipboard content into the Fireworks document.

1 Choose File > Browse in Bridge to switch to Bridge.

2 In Bridge, select the file CityBackground.psd, and then choose File > Open With > Adobe Photoshop CS5 (default).

3 In Photoshop, choose Select > All, and then choose Edit > Copy.

4 Switch back to Fireworks, and then choose Edit > Paste. The background image is inserted into the document Mockup.png.

5 Ensure that the background image is selected. In the Properties panel, set the X and Y offset values to **0**. The image covers the entire document size.

▶ **Tip:** If necessary, you can choose a lower magnification level from the Zoom menu in the lower-right corner of the document panel to see the entire document on your screen.

Using drag and drop

You can drag vector objects, bitmap images, or text directly into a Fireworks document from any application that supports drag and drop—including Photoshop, Illustrator, Flash, and others. You can also drag a file from Bridge or from Windows Explorer/the Finder into the Fireworks document.

1 Choose File > Browse in Bridge to switch to Bridge.

2 Position the Bridge window so that you can see both the Bridge window and the Fireworks document in the background at the same time.

3 From Bridge, drag the file WendyAndMark.psd onto the Fireworks document.

● **Note:** In Windows, if the document window is maximized, you need to click the Restore Down button located beside the Close button in the top-right corner of the document window before you can reposition the window.

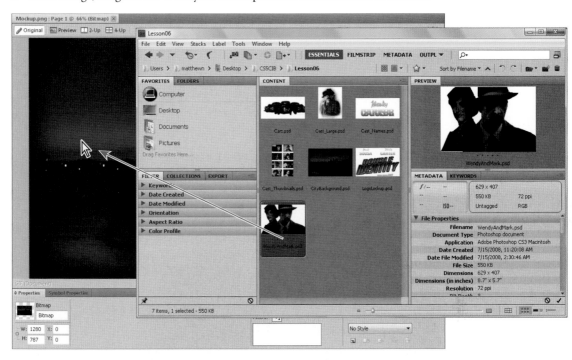

4 In Fireworks, the Photoshop File Import Options dialog box appears. Click OK without making any changes to the default options.

▶ **Tip:** Set the magnification level to 100% from the Zoom menu in the lower-right corner of the document panel so you can position objects more accurately.

5 Drag the placed image toward the top-right corner of the document window. Align the top of the image with the top of the document window and the left edge with the center of the document. Use the smart guides and the X and Y offset values in the Properties panel to guide you.

Applying a gradient mask to a placed image

As you might have noticed, you've just imported not one but two images, each placed on a separate layer. To have these images blend in better with the background, you'll apply a gradient mask to each of them.

▶ **Tip:** The Photoshop File Import Options dialog box gives you the option to flatten a layered Photoshop file to a single-layer image.

1 Choose Select > Deselect. Click to select the image of the man.

2 Choose Commands > Creative > Auto Vector Mask. In the Auto Vector Mask dialog box, select the downward-fading gradient from the Linear options, and then click Apply.

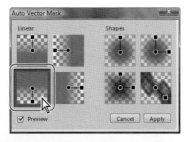

3 Reposition the two handles of the gradient mask so that the fade starts near the man's collar line and ends just below the horizon in the background image.

4 Add a gradient mask for the image of the woman in the same way.

Using the Import command

If you prefer to use a menu command to import images, use the Import command.

1 Choose File > Import.

2 In the Import dialog box, navigate to your Lesson05 folder, select the file Cars. psd, and then click Open.

3 In Fireworks, the Photoshop File Import Options dialog box appears. Click OK without making any changes to the default options. Your pointer changes to a graphics placement cursor (⌐).

4   Click near the center of the background image to place the image of the cars. Drag to position the cars as shown in the following illustration. We set a top-left position of X: **380** and Y: **394** for the group of images.

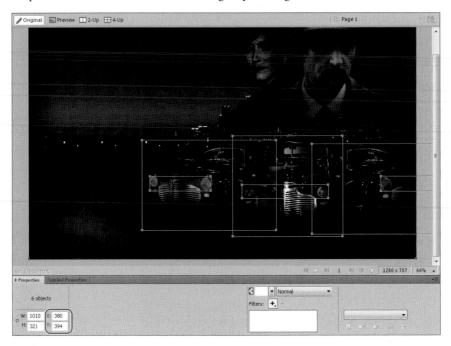

Organizing objects in the Layers panel

The images you've placed so far have been added one above the other and each in its own layer to the Layers panel. Before things get too unwieldy, you should organize your image components into folders in the Layers panel.

1   Choose Select > Deselect.

2   Undock the Layers panel by dragging it out of its panel group, and then resize the panel by dragging its lower-right corner. This will make it easier to work with your layers in the next exercise.

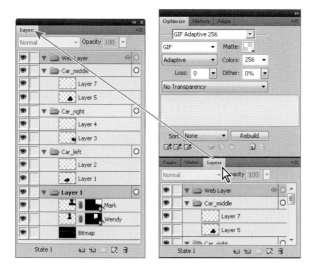

Creating new folders

Try to organize the components in your document by logical groups—the background, the actors, the cars, and so on—and then put each group into its own folder. You'll start by creating a new folder for the images of the actors, which are currently in the same folder as the background image.

1   Select the folder Layer 1 at the bottom of the Layers panel.

2   From the Layers panel Options menu (⚏), located at the right side of the panel header, choose New Layer.

3   In the New Layer dialog box, type **Actors** in the Name text box, disable the Share Across States option, and then click OK.

A new folder, named Actors, is created just above the folder Layer 1.

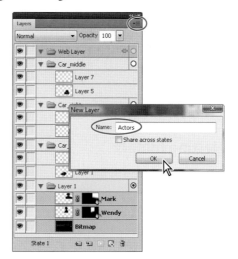

● **Note:** The stacking order of the layers also defines the visibility of objects if they overlap.

● **Note:** You can rearrange layers and folders in the Layers panel by dragging them. Release the pointer when you see the horizontal insertion bar at the desired new location.

Moving objects between and within folders

You can move an object from one folder to another either by simply dragging it or by first selecting the object and then clicking the selection indicator in the destination folder.

▶ **Tip:** If you drop a layer or folder into the wrong location, choose Edit > Undo and try again.

1   Choose Select > Deselect; if the Deselect command is unavailable you don't need to do anything."

2   Drag the layer Mark onto the folder Actors. Release the pointer when you see a black insertion line just below the Actors folder. The layer Mark has been moved inside the Actors folder.

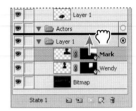

▶ **Tip:** In the Layers panel, you can move multiple selected objects at the same time. Ctrl-click/ Command-click one or more objects, and then move them to a new folder by one of the two methods described above. The original stacking order of the objects will be preserved.

3   Select just the layer Wendy and click the selection indicator in the Actors folder. (See first illustration below.) The layer Wendy has been moved inside the Actors folder and placed above the layer Mark. To reestablish the previous stacking order, drag the layer Wendy below the layer Mark inside the Actors folder. (See second illustration below.)

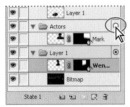

Move Wendy into Actors folder

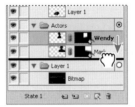

Change order in Actors folder

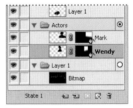

Final arrangement

Nesting folders

Folders can be nested. You'll now create a new folder to hold the three folders for the cars, as shown in the illustration.

1   In the Layers panel, select the folder Car_middle, just below the folder named Web Layer.

2   From the Layers panel Options menu, choose New Layer. In the New Layer dialog box, type **Cars** in the Name text box, disable the Share Across States option, and then click OK.

3   Drag the folder Car_left onto the new Cars folder, followed by the folder Car_right, and finally the folder Car_middle. Don't click the selection indicator in the folder Cars—this would move the selected layers without their parent folder.

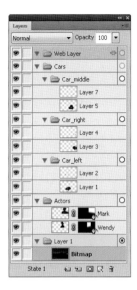

Renaming folders

Giving your folders descriptive names is good organizational practice and helps you keep an overview.

1   Double-click the name of the folder Layer 1 near the bottom of the list in the Layers panel.

2   Type **Background** as the new name, and then press Enter.

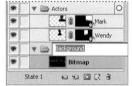

Collapsing and expanding folders; locking and unlocking folders and layers

You can collapse and expand folders to show only the level of detail that currently interests you. Folders and layers you're not currently working with can be locked to avoid unintentional changes.

1   Click the triangles next to the folder names Cars, Actors, and Background to collapse those folders.

2   Click a triangle again to expand a folder.

3   To avoid changing objects unintentionally, click the box in the column immediately to the left of the folder or layer name. A padlock icon (⌂) appears in the box, indicating that the objects in that folder or on that layer are locked.

4   Click the padlock icon to unlock the folder or layer.

5   You can leave the Layers panel undocked for the remainder of this lesson. Alternatively, return the Layers panel to its original location by dragging it by its tab into the same group as the Pages and States panels. To dock the panel in that group, release the mouse button when you see a blue line surrounding the panel group.

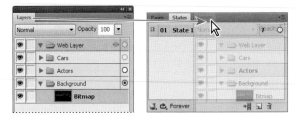

Working with layer comps and flattening images during import

You'll now import a logo lockup into the document from a Photoshop file. A lockup is a set arrangement of a logo together with one or more text elements as defined by the designer. This logo lockup consists of several objects in multiple layers. The file also contains layer comps; during import you can choose which layer comp to import. Because you won't need access to the individual objects in the logo lockup for this exercise, you can flatten the imported layer comp into a single layer in Fireworks.

1   Choose File > Import. In the Import dialog box, navigate to your Lesson05 folder, select the file LogoLockup.psd, and then click Open.

2 In the Photoshop File Import Options dialog box in Fireworks, activate the Show Preview option. Preview each of the available layer comps in the Layer Comps menu in turn; then, select the layer comp Complete_Lockup. From the menu below the Comments pane, choose Flatten Photoshop Layers To Single Image. Activate the option Import Into New Layer. Make sure your settings are exactly as shown in the illustration, and then click OK.

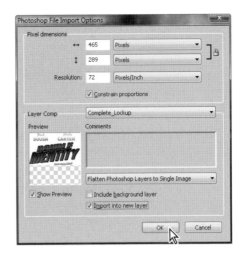

3 The pointer changes to a graphics placement cursor (⌐). Click near the top-left corner of the background image to place the logo image. Drag to reposition the image as shown in the illustration below. We set a top left position of X: **100** and Y: **80** for the image, leaving some space above for the menu bar.

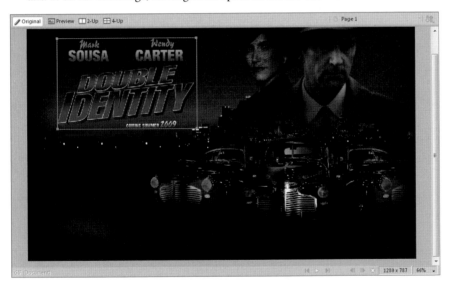

4 Create a new folder above the Cars folder in the Layers panel, name the new folder Logo, and then drag the layer with the newly placed logo image into that folder.

Note: Rich symbols are editable design and interface components that can be used and reused for website designs, interface prototypes, or any other graphic composition.

Adding a navigation bar

Your first page is almost complete. All that's missing is a navigation bar. Fireworks comes with a library of ready-to-use rich symbols, such as interactive buttons and navigation bars.

1   In the Common Library panel (Window > Common Library), scroll down if necessary to see the Menu Bars folder. Click the folder name to expand the folder. Select Menu_Bar_04. You can see a preview of the menu bar design in the area at the top of the Common Library panel.

2   Create a new folder in the Layers panel and name the folder Menu_Bar. Position the new folder just below the folder Web Layer. Click to select the new folder, and then drag Menu_Bar_04 from the Common Library panel onto the Fireworks canvas. In the Layers panel, the menu bar symbol is placed in the folder Menu_Bar.

3   Double-click the new navigation bar on the canvas to enter symbol-editing mode. The other objects on the canvas are dimmed. Note the path to the symbol currently being edited—the symbol Menu_Bar_04 located inside the Page 1—in the tray at the top of the document.

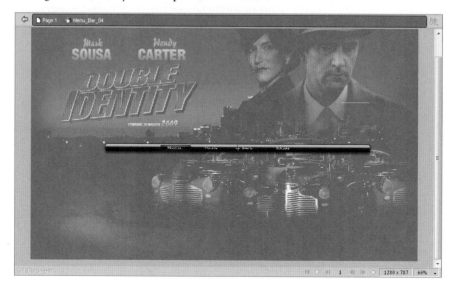

4   In the Layers panel, you can see that this menu bar is composed of six objects—four text layers for the button names, a small rectangle to indicate the currently selected button, and a large background rectangle. Select the large background rectangle in the Layers panel; blue selection handles appear at the corners of the menu bar on the canvas.

5   In the Properties panel, enter **500** in the W (Width) text box and press Enter..

6   Drag the large rectangle to the right on the canvas, holding the Shift key as you drag. Center the rectangle again relative to the four buttons.

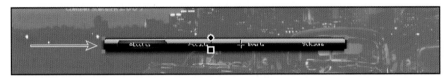

7   In the Tools panel, select the Type tool (**T**). Click inside the text on the About us button to place an insertion cursor. Delete the current text and type **Home**. Rename the remaining buttons in the same way to Actors, Trailer, and Downloads.

8   In the Tools panel, select the Pointer tool (➤). Exit symbol-editing mode by double-clicking outside the navigation bar.

9   Drag the navigation bar to position it near the top of the document, above the logo. Release the pointer when you see the smart guide indicating that the navigation bar is centered above the logo image, as shown in the following illustration. Save your work.

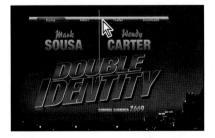

Using a master page

For elements such as a navigation bar that you want to share across all pages, you can create a master page. Elements placed on the master page appear on all the other pages, and subsequent edits made to the master page are reflected on every other page.

Creating a master page

You will now create a new page for the navigation bar and designate it as the master page.

1   In the Pages panel, choose New Page from the panel Options menu to add a new, empty page, named Page 2, to the Pages panel right below Page 1.

2   Select Page 1 in the Pages panel.

3   Click to select the navigation bar on the canvas, and then choose Edit > Cut.

4   Select Page 2 in the Pages panel, and then choose Edit > Paste. The navigation bar is now the only element on page 2.

5   With Page 2 selected in the Pages panel, choose Set As Master Page from the panel Options menu. Page 2 moves to the top of the list in the Pages panel and [Master Page] is added to its name.

6   Select Page 1 in the Pages panel. Note that the navigation bar is not (yet) visible on the canvas. That's because by default the master page elements are added to each page inside a folder called Master Page Layer that is placed right at the bottom of the layer hierarchy. In this example, this layer is hidden behind the background image so you need to move the folder Master Page Layer up in the layer hierarchy to make its elements visible on page 1.

7   In the Layers panel, drag the folder Master Page Layer from the bottom of the list to just below the now empty Menu_Bar folder. If you see an alert warning that a shared layer cannot be made a sublayer, try to reposition the Master Page Layer again, taking special care to release the folder when it's located between the other two folders and not over one of them (which is indicated by the folder icon beside the name turning yellow).

8 Note the padlock icon (🔒) in the column immediately to the left of the Master Page Layer name. You can't unlock this layer from a normal page by clicking the padlock icon; master page objects can only be edited on the master page.

Editing objects on a master page

The navigation bar contains a gradient overlay to give the impression of a depressed button, now indicating the Home page as the current page. Since this gradient overlay needs to be over a different button on each page, you will delete it from the master page and reposition it on page 1.

1 In the Pages panel, select Page 2 [Master Page].

2 Double-click the navigation bar on the canvas to enter symbol-editing mode.

3 Click to select the gradient overlay rectangle over the Home button, being careful not to select the Home button. You should see the blue selection handles at the four corners of the gradient overlay rectangle as well as the two black handles for the gradient. You can also select the gradient overlay rectangle in the Layers panel (the second layer from the bottom).

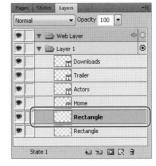

4 Choose Edit > Cut, and then exit symbol-editing mode by double-clicking outside the navigation bar.

5 Note that there is no longer a gradient overlay rectangle visible over the Home button. The change to the master page is reflected in this page..

6 Switch to Page 1 by choosing its name from the Page menu in the top-right corner of the document pane.

7 In the Layers panel, select the empty Menu_Bar folder, and then choose Edit > Paste. The gradient overlay rectangle is placed on a new layer inside the Menu_Bar folder in the Layers panel but off the page in the document window. To move it to where you can see it, enter **200** as X position and **20** as Y position in the Properties panel.

8 Drag the gradient overlay rectangle to center it over the Home text button.

Creating new pages based on the master page

Any pages you add to your document after you have created a master page will inherit the master page settings. You will now create three more pages that will all automatically contain the navigation bar from the master page.

1 In the Pages panel, choose New Page from the panel Options menu three times to create three additional pages. As you add pages note that the navigation bar is automatically placed on each page.

2 Before continuing, it's a good idea to give the pages descriptive names. In the Pages panel, select each page in turn, double-click the page name, and then enter a new name and press Enter. Rename Page 2 to **navbar**—[Master Page] is added automatically—Page 1 to **home**, Page 3 to **actors**, Page 4 to **trailer**, and Page 5 to **downloads**.

To complete the mock-up for the navigation bar and before moving on to make the buttons interactive, you'll place the gradient overlay rectangle over the correct button for each page.

3 In the Pages panel, select the page Home. On the canvas, select the gradient overlay rectangle over the Home button, and then choose Edit > Copy.

4 Switch to the page Actors. In the Layers panel, select the folder just above the Master Page Layer folder, and then choose Edit > Paste.

5 Drag to center the gradient overlay rectangle over the Actors text button. Hold down the Shift key while dragging to restrict the movement to one direction. We set X: **229** and Y: **22** as the position of the top-left corner.

6 Change the trailer and downloads pages accordingly—we set the X positions **348** and **467** respectively, for the two rectangles. When you're done, save your work.

Defining hotspots and linking pages

Hotspots are areas of an image that link to other pages when clicked. To make the navigation bar functional, you'll create hotspots for the four menu buttons and have them link to the appropriate pages.

▶ **Tip:** You can also position objects by entering X and Y values in the Properties panel.

1 In the Pages panel, click each of the four main pages and note how the appearance of the menu bar changes. The visual mock-up of the navigation bar is complete; you'll now add functionality.

2 Select the master page navbar [Master Page].

3 In the Tools panel, select the Rectangle Hotspot tool (🔲), which is grouped with the Circle Hotspot tool (⭕) and the Polygon Hotspot tool (⬡).

4 Using the Rectangle Hotspot tool, drag over the Home button to draw a hotspot area. To reposition the rectangle while dragging, hold down the spacebar.

When you release the mouse button the hotspot area is highlighted over the Home button.

5 With the hotspot rectangle still selected, choose the page home.htm from the Link menu in the Properties panel.

6 Create hotspot areas for the Actors, Trailer, and Downloads buttons in the same way, linking them to the pages actors.htm, trailer.htm, and downloads.htm, respectively.

7 In the Layers panel, note that the four hotspot areas have been created inside the Web Layer folder on the master page. The Web Layer folder appears as the top layer in each document and contains web objects used for adding interactivity to documents exported from Fireworks.

8 Save your work.

Previewing web pages in a web browser

> **Tip:** You can set up both a primary and a secondary web browser to be accessible from the Preview In Browser menu by choosing File > Preview In Browser > Set Primary Browser and File > Preview In Browser > Set Secondary Browser.

1 In the Pages panel, select the page Home. Notice the hotspot areas overlaid over the navigation bar menu buttons. To hide or show hotspots and slice areas while working on your page layout, press 2 on your keyboard or click the Hide Slices And Hotspots button or the Show Slices And Hotspots button in the Tools panel.

A. Hide Slices and Hotspots button
B. Show Slices and Hotspots button

2 To test the functionality of your hotspots, choose File > Preview In Browser > Preview All Pages In [Web Browser Name].

3   In your web browser, move your pointer over the menu buttons. Notice how the pointer changes to the Hand cursor when it's over a hotspot area. Click a menu button to jump to that page.

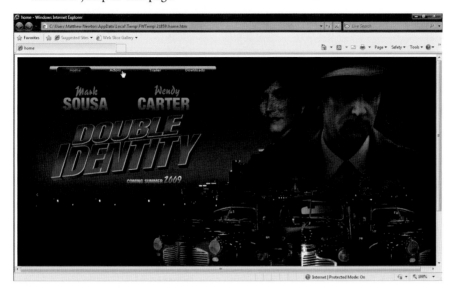

4   You can see which page you're on by the position of the gradient overlay over the menu buttons and by the filename in the address bar.

5   If your links don't work as expected, close the browser window, switch back to Fireworks, and verify that the correct links are specified for the hotspot areas on the master page. Correct any errors, save your changes, and again preview all pages in your web browser.

6   When you've finished testing your navigation bar, close the web browser window and return to Fireworks.

You've completed the mock-up design of the Home page and the navigation bar. Next, you'll work on the Actors page, creating slices and disjoint rollover behaviors.

Sharing layers to pages

You can share a layer across multiple pages in a document. You'll share the background image from the Home page to the Actors page. Unlike elements on a master page, elements on a shared layer can be modified from any page.

1   In the Pages panel, select the page Home.

2   In the Layers panel, select the folder Background. From the Layers panel
    Options menu, choose Share Layer To Pages. In the Share Layer To Pages dialog
    box, select the page Actors in the left column (Exclude Layer From Page(s)), and
    then click Add to add it to the right column (Include Layer To Page(s)).

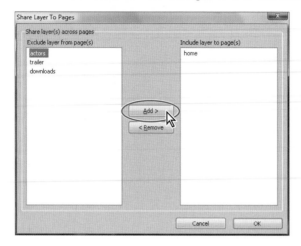

3   Click OK to close the Share Layer To Pages dialog box.

4   Switch to the page Actors and in the Layers panel move the shared Background
    folder to the bottom of the layer list.

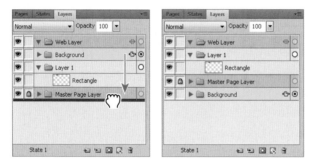

Detaching shared layers

The logo from the Home page should also be placed on the Actors page but should
be scaled down slightly to make more room for other items. To do this, you'll first
share the folder Logo to the page Actors, and then disable the sharing of this layer,
allowing you to modify the object on each page individually.

1   In the Pages panel, select the page Home.

2 In the Layers panel, select the folder Logo. From the Layers panel Options menu, choose Share Layer To Pages. In the Share Layer To Pages dialog box, select the page Actors in the left column and click Add to add it to the right column.

3 Click OK to close the Share Layer To Pages dialog box.

4 Switch to the page Actors and in the Layers panel drag the shared folder Logo between the folders Master Page Layer and Background.

5 With the shared folder Logo selected in the Layers panel, choose Detach Shared Layer from the panel Options menu.

6 Click the Pointer tool in the Tools panel and select the logo artwork on the page Actors. Position the pointer over the lower-right bounding box handle. When the pointer icon changes from filled (▶) to hollow (▷), drag the handle upwards and to the left to reduce the size of the logo image. While dragging, hold down the Shift key to scale the artwork proportionally. Release the mouse button when the width (W) reads 380 in the Properties panel, and then release the Shift key.

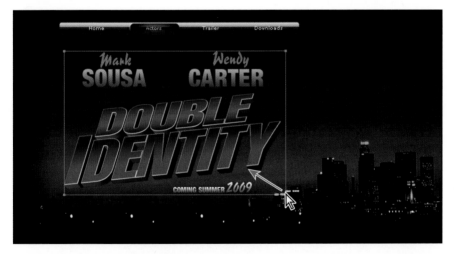

7 Switch to the home page to confirm that the logo placed there didn't change in size, and then switch back to the Actors page.

Creating disjoint rollover behaviors

In the lower-left corner of the Actors page you'll place thumbnail images of the main actors. Moving the pointer over one of the thumbnail images should bring up some text and a large image of the actor in the space to the right of the thumbnails. This is called a disjoint rollover behavior.

Placing the elements

1   In the Layers panel, select the folder Background. Choose New Layer from the panel Options menu. In the New Layer dialog box, type **Actors Thumbnails** in the Name text box, and then click OK.

2   Choose File > Import. In the Import dialog box, navigate to your Lesson05 folder, select the file Cast_Thumbnails.psd, and then click Open.

3   In the Photoshop File Import Options dialog box, leave the default settings and make sure Maintain Layer Editability Over Appearance is selected in the menu below the Comments field.

4   Your cursor changes to a graphics placement cursor (⌐). Click near the left edge of the background image to place the thumbnail images. Drag to reposition the thumbnail images as shown in the following illustration. We set a top-left position of X: 100 and Y: 444 for the group of images.

5   Select New Layer from the Layers panel Options menu. In the New Layer dialog box, type **Actors Large Images** in the Name text box, and then click OK.

6   Choose File > Import. In the Import dialog box, select the Photoshop file Cast_Large.psd, and then click Open. In the Photoshop File Import Options dialog box, choose Last Document State from the Layer Comp menu, choose Maintain Layer Editability Over Appearance from the menu below, activate the option Include Background Layer, disable the option Import Into New Layer, and then click OK. Your cursor changes to a graphics placement cursor (⌐).

7   Click near the center of the background image to place the large images. Drag, use the arrow keys, or enter X and Y values directly in the Properties panel to reposition the large images. We set a top left position of X: 550 and Y: 400 for the group of images.

8   Select New Layer from the panel Options menu. In the New Layer dialog box, type **Actors Names** in the Name text box, and then click OK.

9   Choose File > Import. In the Import dialog box, select the file Cast_Names.psd, and then click Open. In the Photoshop File Import Options dialog box, choose Last Document State from the Layer Comp menu, choose Maintain Layer Editability Over Appearance from the menu below, activate the option Include Background Layer, disable the option Import Into New Layer, and then click OK. Your cursor changes to a graphics placement cursor (⌐).

10 Place the name graphics between the thumbnails images and the large images. We set a top-left position of X: 340 and Y: 420 for the group of images. Your page should now look like the following illustration.

11 Save your work.

Using dummy text

For the purpose of a website mock-up you'll normally use dummy text to show how text will look on the page.

▶ **Tip:** You can format and style the dummy text using the controls in the Properties panel.

1 Select New Layer from the Layers panel Options menu. In the New Layer dialog box, type **Actors Text** as the folder name, and then click OK.

2 Choose Commands > Text > Lorem ipsum. A text frame filled with dummy text appears on the page. With the text frame still selected, make sure the text color is white using the color picker for Fill Color in the Tools panel or the Properties panel.

3 To reposition the text box, enter the following values in the Properties panel: X: **340** and Y: **520**.

4 Position your pointer over the lower-right bounding box handle. When the pointer changes from filled (▶) to hollow (▷), drag the handle downwards and to the left. Release the pointer when the width (W) reads 206 and the height (H) reads 192 in the Properties panel.

Creating slices

The disjoint rollover effect works by swapping images inside defined slice areas on the page. You'll create slices for the actors names, the large images, and the dummy text.

1 Right-click/Control-click the text frame containing the dummy text, and then choose Insert Slice from the menu.

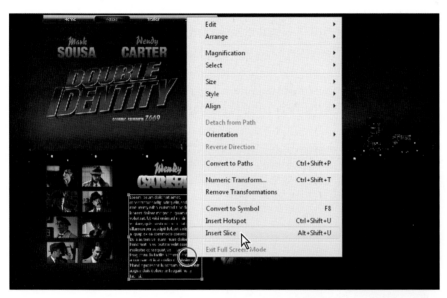

2 In the Layers panel, turn on the visibility of the layer Background inside the folder Actors Names. A gray rectangle appears behind the actors names in the document window. Right-click/Control-click near the edge of that gray rectangle, being careful not to click too closely to the actors names. You should see a blue selection rectangle around the gray rectangle. Choose Insert Rectangular Slice from the menu.

3 In the Layers panel, turn on the visibility of the layer Layer 5 inside the layer Actors Large Images. A gray rectangle appears behind the actors images in the document. Right-click/Control-click near the edge of that gray rectangle—being careful not to click to closely to the actors images; you should see a blue selection rectangle the size of the gray rectangle—and then choose Insert Rectangular Slice from the menu.

4 You've created three slices that have all been added to the Web Layer in the Layers panel.

▶ **Tip:** You can now delete the two gray rectangles to avoid clutter in the Layers panel; the gray rectangles were only added to the Photoshop file to make it easier to define the dimensions of the slices in Fireworks.

Adding states

Pages can have multiple states; for example: the normal state, the state when the pointer moves over the first hotspot with a rollover behavior, the state when the pointer moves over the second hotspot with a rollover behavior, and so on. States can also be used to implement frame animations. For this exercise, you'll design just two extra states for the page; doing more is possible but doesn't add anything essential to the website mock-up.

1 In the States panel, confirm that there is currently only one state, State 1, which is selected by default.

2 With State 1 selected in the States panel, turn off the visibility of the folders Actors Text, Actors Names, and Actors Large Images. Click the Hide Slices And Hotspots button in the Tools panel to see the page as it would appear in the normal state.

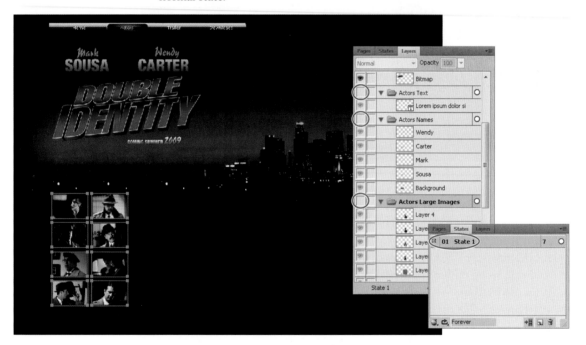

3 In the States panel, choose Duplicate State from the panel Options menu. In the Duplicate State dialog box, type **2** in the Number text box, select the After Current State option, and then click OK.

4 If it's not already selected, select State 2 in the States panel. For this state you'll design how the page will look when the pointer moves over the first actor's thumbnail image.

5   In the Layers panel, turn on the visibility of the folders Actors Text, Actors
    Names, and Actors Large Images. Within the folder Actors Names turn off the
    visibility of all but the two layers Wendy and Carter. Within the folder Actors
    Large Images turn off the visibility for all but Layer 1, as shown here.

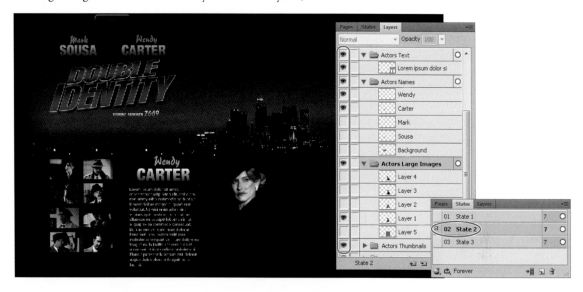

6   Select State 3 in the States panel. For this state you'll design how the page will
    look when the pointer moves over the second actor's thumbnail image.

7   In the Layers panel, turn on the visibility of the folders Actors Text, Actors
    Names, and Actors Large Images. Within the folder Actors Names turn off the
    visibility of all but the two layers Mark and Sousa. Within the folder Actors Large
    Images turn off the visibility for all but the one layer Layer 2, as shown here.

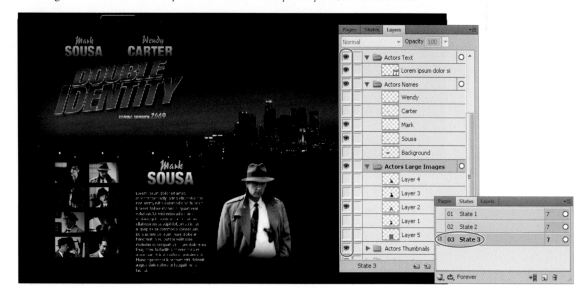

8 Save your work.

You've completed the design for the three states of your Actors page. In the next steps you'll define the hotspot areas and attach disjoint rollover behaviors.

Creating hotspot areas and attaching disjoint rollover behaviors

Moving the pointer over the first thumbnail image should trigger the images you've placed in State 2 to appear in the three slices. You'll place a hotspot area over the first thumbnail image and then attach a disjoint rollover behavior, which will swap an image in a slice area. You can swap images in more than one slice at the same time by attaching additional disjoint rollover behaviors.

1 Select State 1 in the States panel.

2 Right-click/Control-click the top-left thumbnail image, and then choose Insert Hotspot from the menu.

3 Drag the behavior handle (⊕) from the hotspot area onto the first target slice.

4 In the Swap Image dialog box that appears when you release the mouse button, choose State 2 from the Swap Image From menu, and then click OK.

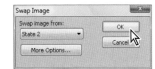

5 Repeat steps 3 and 4 twice to create two more disjoint rollover behaviors for the hotspot area over the top-left thumbnail image—one for the slice containing the large image and one for the slice containing the dummy text. Both times, choose State 2 from the Swap Image From menu in the Swap Image dialog box, and then click OK.

6 Create a hotspot area over the top-right thumbnail image and attach a disjoint rollover behavior for each of the three slice areas, each time choosing State 3 from the Swap Image From menu in the Swap Image dialog box. When a hotspot is selected, blue behavior lines indicate the connection between the hotspot and the controlled slice areas.

7 Save your work.

8 Choose File > Preview In Browser > Preview In [Web Browser Name].

9 In your web browser, position your pointer over each of the thumbnail images to test the disjoint rollover behaviors.

10 Close your web browser window and return to Fireworks.

Presenting the prototype website to the client

There are many ways in which you can demonstrate the prototype website to your client—many more than we can explore here. You may settle for only one of the methods described here or use several methods in combination.

Exporting the website as a PDF document

Fireworks enables you to export your website prototype as a high-fidelity, interactive, secure PDF document that you can use in an e-mail based or online review process.

1 Choose File > Export.

2 In the Export dialog box, navigate to your Lesson05 folder, choose Adobe PDF from the Export menu, choose All Pages from the Pages menu, and select the View PDF After Export option.

3 (Optional) Click Options to specify compatibility and image quality settings or to set up password protection for the PDF.

4 Click Save/Export.

Fireworks generates a PDF version of your website and then opens the document in your default PDF viewer.

5 Navigate through the pages using any of the regular page navigation controls. Alternatively, click the menu buttons of the navigation bar inside the document to jump directly to the corresponding pages. Note that in a PDF document you will not be able to preview rollover effects such as those you created on the Actors page.

6 Close the PDF document and return to Fireworks.

Creating an auto-run slide show

To present the pages of your website as a slide show without the need for user interaction, use the Demo Current Document command.

1 Choose Commands > Demo Current Document.

Tip: To create a subfolder while you're in the Folder For Export dialog box, do one of the following: On Windows, right-click the file list pane and choose New > Folder from the menu. On Mac OS, click the New Folder button.

2 In the Demo Current Document dialog box, deselect the box for the master page navbar, set the background color to black by typing **#000000** in the color text box or by using the color picker beside it, and then click Create Demo. In the Folder For Export dialog box, navigate to your Lesson05 folder— optionally, you could create a subfolder inside the Lesson05 folder—and then click Select [Folder name]/Choose.

3 After the export is complete, your default web browser opens and automatically begins displaying the pages of your website as a slide show. Move the pointer towards the lower edge of the browser window to see the navigation controls. You can stop the playback or switch to full-screen mode. Note that once again you can't preview the rollover effects.

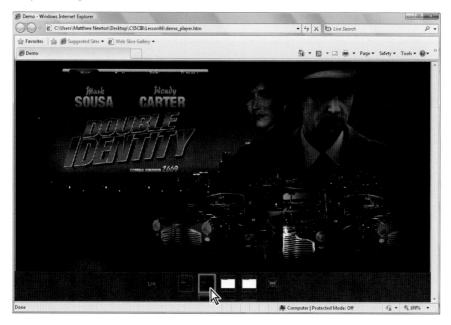

4 When you're done reviewing the slide show, close the web browser window and return to Fireworks.

Exporting states of a page as individual images

When demonstrating complex rollover behaviors, you might want to take snapshots of the various states of a page as individual images.

1 Switch to the page actors.

2 Choose File > Export.

3 In the Export dialog box, navigate to your Lesson05 folder—optionally, you could create a subfolder inside the Lesson05 folder—choose States To Files from the Export menu, and then click Save/Export.

▶ **Tip:** To create a subfolder while you're in the Export dialog box, do one of the following: On Windows, right-click the file list pane and choose New > Folder from the menu. On Mac OS, click the New Folder button.

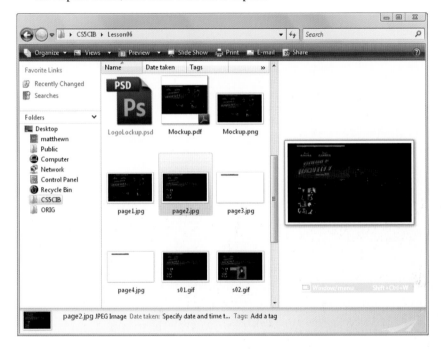

Fireworks generates one image for each state of the current page. You can review the images in Windows Explorer/the Finder or in any image-processing application.

Exporting HTML pages

Probably the best way to demonstrate a website mock-up is to actually export a working website prototype. Fireworks can generate HTML pages and images directly from the Fireworks document—complete with functional navigation bar and rollover behaviors.

1 Choose File > Export.

2 In the Export dialog box, navigate to your Lesson05 folder.

3   Create a subfolder inside the Lesson05 folder: On Windows, right-click the file list pane and choose New > Folder. On Mac OS, click the New Folder button. Name the new folder html_export.

4   Navigate to the newly created subfolder inside the Lesson05 folder. In the Export dialog box, choose HTML And Images from the Export menu. Choose Export HTML File from the HTML menu and Export Slices from the Slices menu. Choose All Pages from the Pages menu. Select the option Include Areas Without Slices and deselect the Current State Only option.

5   Select the option Put Images In Subfolder. By default, this will place all images in a folder named images inside the selected folder, which is suitable for our purposes.

6   Confirm that everything looks exactly as shown in the following illustration, and then click Save/Export.

7   When the export is complete, switch to Windows Explorer/the Finder. Navigate to the html_export subfolder inside the Lesson05 folder and double-click the file home.htm. The page opens in your default web browser.

8 Test the functionality of the navigation bar by clicking on its menu buttons. You should be able to jump from each page directly to any other page. Navigate to the Actors page and move the pointer over the two top thumbnail images. You should be able to see the disjoint rollover behaviors you created in Fireworks.

Your website mock-up is ready for review by your client or colleagues. You can upload the content of the html_export folder onto a web server and point your client to it. Or, you could demonstrate the functionality of the website in an online meeting. See Lesson 8, "Submitting Work for a PDF Review," for more information about collaborating in online meetings using Share My Screen and Connect Now. Once you've obtained your client's approval on the design it's time to build the website in Dreamweaver, reusing the work you've done in Fireworks.

Building a website in Dreamweaver

The tight integration between Fireworks and Dreamweaver makes it very easy to create a Dreamweaver website from assets created in Fireworks. Simply export the elements you want to use from your Fireworks document, and then insert them into your Dreamweaver document. From the assets exported from the Fireworks document, you can pick and choose the elements you want to use: images, entire tables containing sliced graphics, individual rollover buttons or ready-to-use navigation bars, complete web pages with all elements already positioned, or any combination thereof.

Creating a new site

You'll begin by creating a new site in Dreamweaver. Part of the site creation process is to define a location on your hard disk where all the pages and images for your new website will be stored. This location is referred to as the local root folder for your Dreamweaver site.

1 Launch Adobe Dreamweaver CS5.

2 Click the Dreamweaver Site button under Create New in the Welcome screen, or choose Site > New Site.

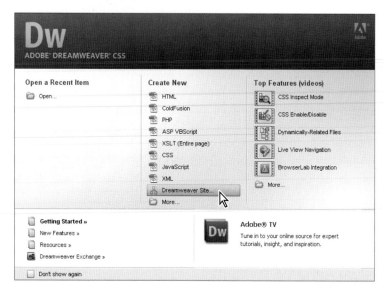

3 In the Site Definition dialog box, type **Double Identity Site** in the site name text box. (See illustration on next page.)

4 Click the Browse button beside Local Site Folder. Navigate to your Lesson05 folder. Create a new folder called Website inside the Lesson05 folder. Open the new Website folder, and then click Select/Choose.

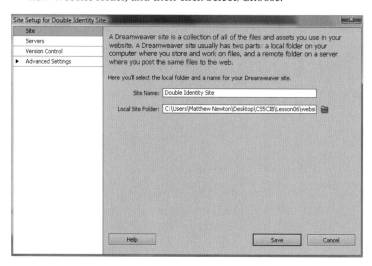

5 Click Save in the Site Setup dialog box.

5 Your new site is added to the Files panel where you can easily access and organize all the files that make up your website.

Creating new pages with CSS styles

You will now add blank HTML pages to your website into which you will place the HTML pages exported from Fireworks. The Dreamweaver pages will serve as containers for the Fireworks pages. The CSS style attached to the Dreamweaver pages will keep the placed images horizontally centered in the web browser window when the window is enlarged.

1 Choose File > New.

2 In the New Document dialog box, select the Blank Page category, if necessary, from the first column. In the Page Type column, select HTML. In the Layout column, select 1 Column Liquid, Centered; then click Create.

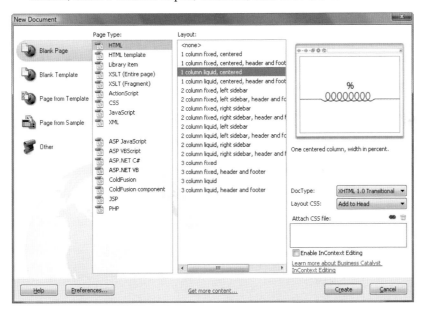

3 Choose File > Save As. In the Save As dialog box, click the Site Root button, type **home.htm** in the File Name/Save As text box, and then click Save.

This simple web page layout has a CSS (Cascading Style Sheets) class named container assigned to a single DIV (page division) inside the body of the page. If this is starting to sound confusing, don't worry. We won't dive deep into the topic of CSS. For now it's only important to understand that using CSS separates page content from page layout. For example, the style definition of the class container establishes that the content of the page (inside the container) remains horizontally centered on the page. You could easily change the content to be left aligned, for example, by editing the style definition. No change is necessary to the content of the page.

Inspecting CSS-based page elements

While you edit your web page in Code view, Dreamweaver presents the CSS properties for the current HTML tag in the CSS Styles panel.

1 In Code view, click to place the cursor inside the <body> tag.

2 In the CSS Styles panel, notice that the properties shown are specific to the page's body.

3 In Code view, click to place the cursor inside the <div class="container"> tag.

4 In the CSS Styles panel, notice that the properties shown are now specific to the container class.

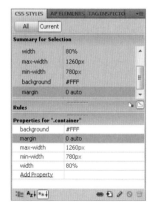

Inserting Fireworks HTML pages

You'll replace the entire content of the DIV container with the HTML page exported from Fireworks. You'll begin by setting the width of the container to the width of the HTML page it should contain.

1   Click anywhere in the dummy text of the home.htm page in Dreamweaver.

2   At the bottom of the document view, click the tag <div.container>, and then click the CSS Panel button in the Properties panel.

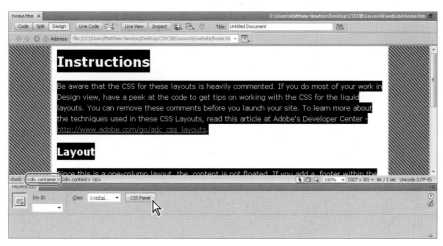

3   In the CSS Styles panel, double-click the Width property to open the CSS Rule Definition dialog box. Type **1280** in the Width text box and choose px (pixels) from the units menu beside it. Click OK to close the dialog box.

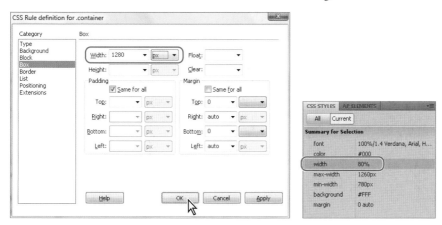

4 In Code view, select everything between the tags <div class="container"> and <!-- end .container --></div>, and then choose Insert > Image Objects > Fireworks HTML.

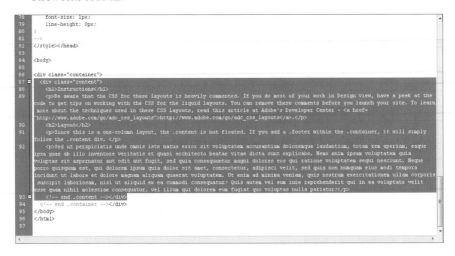

5 In the Insert Fireworks HTML dialog box, click the Browse button to locate the Fireworks HTML file you want to insert. In the Select The Fireworks HTML File dialog box, navigate to the html_export folder inside your Lesson05 folder, select the file home.htm, and then click Open. Deselect the option Delete File After Insertion, and then click OK to close the Insert Fireworks HTML dialog box.

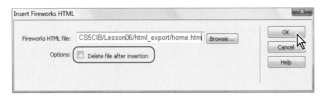

6 In the warning dialog box, click OK to copy referenced files into the site folder. It is recommended that you move all files related to the website inside the local root folder. You could also have created the website in Dreamweaver first, and then exported the HTML pages from Fireworks into the local root folder.

7 In the Copy Image Files To dialog box, navigate to the local root folder website, create a new folder inside that folder and name it **Images**, open the new Images folder, and then click Select/Choose.

8 In the CSS Styles panel, click the Refresh button to view your updated content in the document pane.

9 Choose File > Save and then choose File > Preview In Browser > [Web Browser Name]. The page opens in your default web browser. If your computer screen is large enough, enlarge the width of the browser window and note that the image stays centered within the browser window. Later in this lesson you will change the background color of the page to black so the image blends perfectly into the background.

10 Close the browser window and return to Dreamweaver.

Roundtrip editing between Dreamweaver and Fireworks

The web page consists of a single large GIF image and an image map for the hotspot areas of the navigation bar. To edit the image, if necessary, you can take advantage of the tight cross-product integration between Fireworks and Dreamweaver: In Fireworks, edit the original file in PNG format, which was used to generate the Fireworks HTML pages and have the changes incorporated automatically when you return to Dreamweaver.

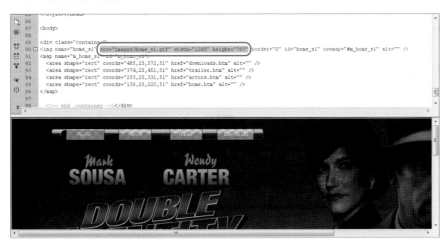

To enable roundtrip editing for the main image in GIF file format on our Home page, shown in Design view and also circled in Code view in the figure above, Fireworks needs to be set as the primary external editor for GIF images in Dreamweaver. This can be done in Dreamweaver Preferences.

Setting Fireworks as primary editor for GIF images

Fireworks can register itself as the primary editor for GIF images on your system. Opening GIFs in Windows Explorer or the Mac Finder will then cause Fireworks to launch.

1 Choose Edit > Preferences/Dreamweaver > Preferences.

2 Select File Types/Editors from the Category list.

3 Select .gif from the Extensions list.

4 Select Fireworks from the Editors list, and then click the Make Primary button.

5 With Fireworks set as primary editor for .gif images, click OK to close the Preferences dialog box.

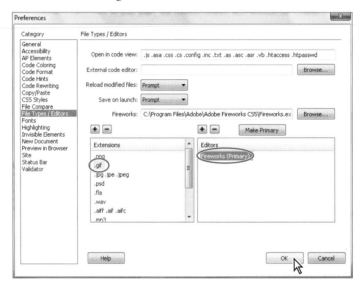

Edit the original PNG file of a GIF image placed in Dreamweaver

Changes made to a source PNG file in Fireworks can flow automatically into Dreamweaver. Here we'll update a GIF image by editing our original Fireworks PNG.

1 In Design view, right-click/Control-click anywhere in the main image in the Design view in Dreamweaver and choose Edit With > Adobe Fireworks CS5.

2 In the Find Source dialog box, click the Use A PNG button.

3 In the Open/Open File dialog box, navigate to the Lesson05 folder, select the file Mockup.png, and then click Open.

4 Fireworks opens the PNG file in a special editing window, which is indicated by an additional bar across the top of the window. If you see an alert about the structure of the HTML table, click OK.

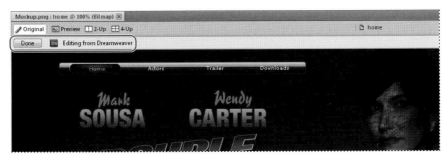

5   Make sure you're on page 1; if necessary, click 01 home in the Pages panel. In the Layers panel, expand the folder Cars, if necessary. Turn off the visibility of Layer 2 inside the subfolder Car_left and Layer 4 inside the subfolder Car_right. Select Layer 7 inside the subfolder Car_middle and change the layer opacity to about 80%. These changes will turn on the headlights of the three cars.

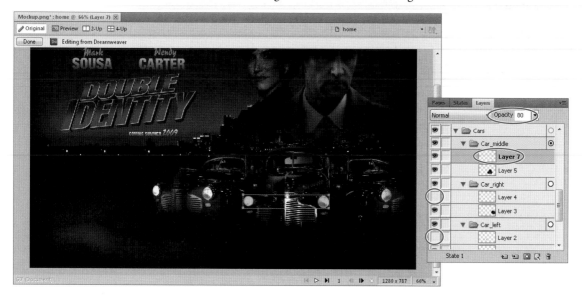

6   Click Done in the bar across the top of the editing window to save your edits to the image, close the file, and return to Dreamweaver.

The GIF image used for the Home page in Dreamweaver is automatically updated to reflect the edits you made to the PNG document.

Wrapping up

To complete this lesson, you'll change the background color of the Home page to black and then use that page as a starting point for your work on the Actors page.

Changing the page background color

1   In Dreamweaver, click the tag <body> at the bottom of the document view.

2   In the CSS Styles panel, double-click the property background to open the CSS
    Rule Definition dialog box. Type **#000000** in the Background-color text box or
    click the color swatch beside it and use the color picker to set the background
    color to black. Click OK to close the dialog box.

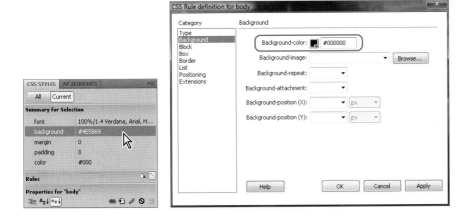

Creating new pages using the current page settings

To create the Actors page, you can use a copy of the Home page and then replace
the content of the container.

1   Choose File > Save As. In the Save As dialog box, click the Site Root button,
    type **actors.htm** in the File Name/Save As text box, and then click Save.

2 The new page is added to the list of files in the Files panel.

3 In Code view, select everything between the tags <div class="container"> and <!-- end .container --></div>, as shown in the following illustration, and then choose Insert > Image Objects > Fireworks HTML.

```
86   </head>
87
88   <body><div class="container">
89   <img name="home_s1" src="images/home_s1.gif" width="1280" height="787" border="0" id="home_s1" usemap="#m_home_s1" alt="" /><map
     name="m_home_s1" id="m_home_s1">
90   <area shape="rect" coords="485,25,572,51" href="downloads.htm" alt="" />
91   <area shape="rect" coords="374,25,451,51" href="trailer.htm" alt="" />
92   <area shape="rect" coords="253,25,331,51" href="actors.htm" alt="" />
93   <area shape="rect" coords="130,25,220,51" href="home.htm" alt="" />
94   <area shape="rect" coords="485,25,572,51" href="downloads.htm" alt="" />
95   <area shape="rect" coords="374,25,451,51" href="trailer.htm" alt="" />
96   <area shape="rect" coords="253,25,331,51" href="actors.htm" alt="" />
97   <area shape="rect" coords="130,25,220,51" href="home.htm" alt="" />
98   </map>
99
100      <!-- end .container --></div>
101  </body>
102  </html>
```

4 In the Insert Fireworks HTML dialog box, click the Browse button. In the Select The Fireworks HTML File dialog box, navigate to the html_export folder inside your Lesson05 folder, select the file actors.htm, and then click Open. Deselect the option Delete File After Insertion, and then click OK to close the Insert Fireworks HTML dialog box.

5 In the warning dialog box, click OK to copy referenced files into the site folder. In the Copy Image Files To dialog box, navigate to the Images folder inside the local root folder website, and then click Select/Choose.

6 In the CSS Styles panel, click the Refresh button to view your updated content in the document pane.

7 Save your document.

Reviewing the disjoint rollover behavior

The Actors page contains hotspot areas with disjoint rollover behaviors. You can use the Tag Inspector in Dreamweaver to review—or, if necessary, add, delete, or modify—the behaviors for the hotspot areas on the page.

1 In Design view, click to select the hotspot area over the top-left thumbnail image.

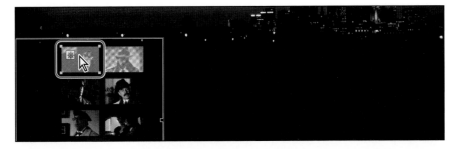

2 Choose Window > Behaviors to open the Behaviors tab of the Tag Inspector. Double-click Swap Image beside the onMouseOver behavior to open the Swap Image dialog box.

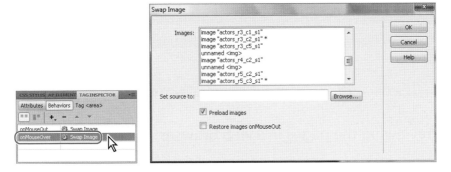

3 In the Images list, start from the top and slowly scroll down. One at a time, select each entry with an asterisk (*) behind its name, such as the entry for image "actors_r2_c6_s1" * in the following illustration. The individual images are the slices that make up the entire page. With the "actors_r2_c6_s1" * entry selected, the currently defined replacement image (or slice) is listed as images/actors_r2_c6_s2.jpg in the Set Source To text box.

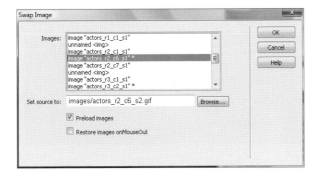

4 Click OK to close the Swap Image dialog box.

5 You can verify the name of a slice and the name of the image that will be displayed in that slice in the page's normal state by clicking to select the slice in Design view.

Previewing the pages in a web browser

The only way to know for certain your work will display ideally in a browser is to open the browser.

1 Choose File > Save, and then choose File > Preview In Browser > [Web Browser Name]. Depending on the security settings on your computer you may first need to allow blocked content before you can display the page.

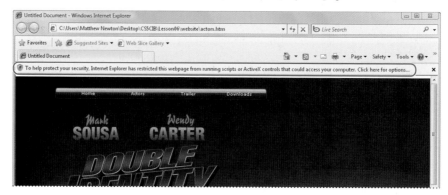

2 The page opens in your default web browser.

3 Click the Home and Actors buttons in the navigation bar to switch between the two pages you've created so far.

4 If your computer screen is large enough, enlarge the width of the browser window and note that the background color of the page is now black so the image blends perfectly into the background.

5 On the Actors page, move the pointer over the top two thumbnail images to test the disjoint rollover behavior.

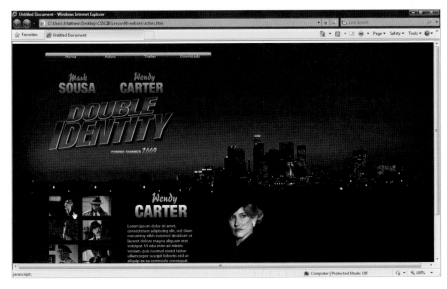

6 When you're done reviewing, close the browser window and return to Dreamweaver.

This completes our brief introduction to Fireworks and Dreamweaver.

To complete the website, you would remove the dummy text on the Actors page in Fireworks and create an absolute positioned text frame at the same location in Dreamweaver. Enter the final version of the text provided by the client and add a show/hide behavior to the hotspots over the thumbnail images. The text can then be styled and formatted to your liking—or your client's—using CSS style sheets, including attributes such as type style, size, color, alignment, and margins.

Needless to say you'd have to add more images and hotspots, and you would also need to complete the two remaining pages.

Finally, you'd upload the pages directly from Dreamweaver to a remote web server.

Review questions

1 Describe the typical workflow for development of a website using Fireworks and Dreamweaver.

2 What is the reasoning behind building a rapid prototype of the website as the first stage of website development?

3 Name three methods for placing images in a Fireworks document.

4 What is a master page used for in Fireworks?

5 How do you use slices and states to implement a rollover behavior?

6 Explain roundtrip editing between Dreamweaver and Fireworks.

Review answers

1 Designing a website from start to finish follows this basic workflow:

   • Together with the client, define the scope of the project, including the objectives of the website, the target audience, schedule, and available resources.

   • Develop a design strategy and establish the look and feel of the web pages.

   • Create a prototype of the website in Fireworks.

   • Present the design to the client and refine it as necessary to obtain approval.

   • Assemble the required assets and create the website in Dreamweaver, based on the work done in Fireworks.

2 Since the creation of an entire website is quite labor intensive it is essential that you agree with your client on the design direction very early on in the project using the rapid prototyping capabilities of Fireworks. Best of all, all the work that goes into the development of the website mock-up can later be reused for the actual implementation of the website.

3 You can place images in a Fireworks document using drag and drop, copy and paste, or the Import command.

4 For elements that you want to share across all pages, such as a common background image or a navigation bar, you can create a master page. Elements placed on the master page and any edits made to the master page subsequently are reflected on all other pages.

5   Create a slice the size of the area where you want the image to change for the rollover behavior. Place the rollover state image inside the slice area but on a different state of the page. Attach a rollover behavior from another slice or a hotspot to the new slice, and select the swap image from the appropriate state of the page.

6   An image that was exported from Fireworks and then placed in Dreamweaver can be edited by opening the PNG file from which the image was created in Fireworks, making the adjustments, and then reexporting and placing the image in Dreamweaver. This process is automated if you follow these steps:

    •   To set Fireworks as the primary image editor for the relevant image format, choose Edit With > Fireworks from within Dreamweaver.

    •   Select the original PNG image when prompted.

    •   Edit the image in Fireworks.

6 CREATING ANIMATED FLASH CONTENT

Lesson Overview

In this lesson, you'll learn the Flash Professional skills and techniques you need to create an animated website from a design created in Fireworks.

- Creating a Flash document

- Importing artwork created in Fireworks

- Adding simple animations

- Defining rollover behaviors

- Using ActionScript

- Publishing for a web browser and Flash Player

- Creating an AIR application

 This lesson will take about two hours to complete.

Import the website prototype created in Fireworks into a Flash document. Add animation and special effects. Use ActionScript to control media elements behaviors. Test and publish your document.

Note: Before you start working on this lesson, make sure that you've installed the Creative Suite 5 Design Premium software on your computer, and that you have correctly copied the Lessons folder from the CD in the back of this book onto your computer's hard disk (see "Copying the Classroom in a Book files" on page 2).

About Adobe Flash Professional CS5

Adobe Flash Professional is the tool of choice to add animation and interactivity to your documents. The Flash Platform delivers the most effective immersive experiences for rich content, applications, and communications across browsers, operating systems, and devices of all kinds.

A typical workflow

To create an interactive document in Flash, you typically perform the following steps:

1   Plan the animations and how the user should interact with your document.

2   Create assets and import them to your Flash document.

3   Arrange the elements on the Stage and the Timeline to define when and how they appear in your document.

4   Add special effects and interactivity.

5   Test and publish your document.

Since Flash is such a powerful tool it can be intimidating to work with at first. To give you an indication of the degree of interactivity you can achieve by using some advanced Flash development features, we've provided a relatively complex version of a website design in the Lesson06 folder. Throughout this lesson you will be working on a simpler version of the home page that teaches the concepts of working with Flash without adding too much complexity. Where appropriate, implementation differences between the simple and the complex design will be pointed out.

Viewing the complex sample document

You will start by opening an animated Flash website, which is provided in the Lesson06 folder. You can keep this website open as a reference while working on a simpler version of the home page.

Tip: To show the filename extensions in Windows Explorer, do the following: Choose Tools > Folder Options, click the View tab and under Advanced Settings, deselect the Hide Extensions For Known File Types option.

1   In Windows Explorer/the Finder, navigate to your Lesson06 folder. Within that folder open the Double Identity folder. Double-click the file index_flash.html; it opens in your default web browser.

2   In your web browser, watch the intro animation of the home page: The images fade in and slide into position. When the animation stops, move your pointer over one of the cars. The car bounces slightly up and down and the headlights go on. Move the pointer away and the car animation stops.

3   Feel free to explore the other pages of this Flash movie. Click the CAST & CREW button at the top of the page. Click the VIDEO button in the navigation bar to open a page showing a movie trailer. Use the playback controls below the movie trailer to stop playback. Click the logo image to return to the home page and watch the intro animation play again.

You can leave the web browser open if you want; otherwise, close the browser window. Next you'll open the Flash document that was used to create this Flash movie.

4   Start Adobe Flash Professional CS5.

▶ **Tip:** If you missed parts of the opening animation and want to see them again, click the Reload button in your web browser.

5 Click the Open button in the Welcome screen, or choose File > Open.

6 In the Open dialog box, navigate to your Lesson06 folder. Open the folder Double Identity. Within that folder select the file index.fla, and then click Open.

If a Font Mapping dialog box appears because you might not have all fonts used in the document installed on your system, click Cancel. For the purpose of this exercise you will not need to worry about font mappings.

The document opens in Flash. However, you will only see a black page on the Stage area, and the Timeline contains only one frame with two layers. Later in this lesson you'll discover where all the content is hidden. For now, just leave the document open while you're creating a new document from scratch.

Creating a Flash document

You will create a simple version of the home page using the Fireworks mockup document from Lesson05 as starting point, and then add some animation and interactivity to the document.

1   Choose File > New, and then double-click ActionScript 3.0 in the New Document
    dialog box.

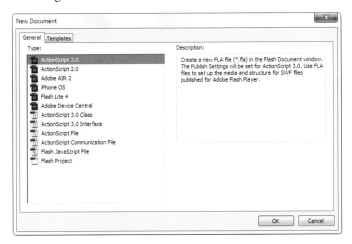

2   In the Properties panel (Window > Properties), expand the Properties pane, if
    necessary, and click the Edit button in that pane—not to be confused with the
    Edit buttons in the Publish pane—to open the Document Properties dialog box.

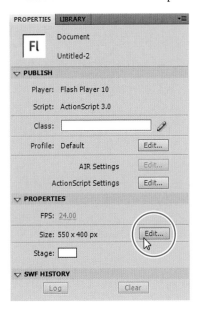

3 In the Document Properties dialog box, type **1280 px** in the Width text box and **787 px** in the Height text box. These are the dimensions used for the prototype document created in Fireworks that you will later place onto the Stage in Fireworks. Click the color swatch next to Background Color and set the color to black in the color picker. Type **12** fps (frames per second) in the Frame Rate text box, and then click OK.

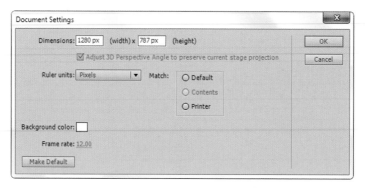

▶ **Tip:** For content intended for onscreen viewing in a web browser, do not use a frame rate higher than 8–12 fps to avoid heavy CPU usage during playback.

4 To see the entire content of the Stage in the document window, choose View > Magnification > Fit In Window, or choose Fit In Window from the Magnification menu located in the upper-right corner of the document window.

Placing images

Flash supports importing of vector and bitmap images in a variety of file formats. You can import artwork directly onto the Stage or only to the Library to position it later on the Stage. In this exercise you'll import the website prototype you've created in Fireworks in Lesson05, preserving all layers and the image composition.

1 Choose File > Import > Import To Stage.

2 In the Import dialog box, navigate to your Lesson06 folder, select the file Mockup.png, and then click Open/Import.

3 In the Import Fireworks Document dialog box, deselect the Import As A Single Flattened Bitmap option. From the Import menu, choose the page *home*. From the Into menu, choose Current Frame As Movie Clip. For both Objects and Text, select the options to maintain appearance when importing, and then click OK.

Note: When importing a Fireworks PNG file as a single flattened bitmap, you can roundtrip edit the image from Flash to Fireworks and back to Flash—but you can't animate individual components of the image in Flash.

The image is placed on the Stage. Frame 1 of Layer 1 in the Timeline contains one element: the entire home page converted into a single movie clip.

4 Double-click the image on the Stage to enter symbol-editing mode. Note the path to the symbol currently being edited—the movie clip home in Scene 1— in the Edit bar at the top of the document.

Note: A symbol is a graphic, button, or movie clip organized in the Library panel. You can place multiple instances of a symbol on the Stage. Each symbol has its own Timeline, where you can add layers, frames, and ActionScript code to create animations and behaviors for the symbol.

The Timeline shows all layers and objects included in this movie clip. You may need to scroll down in the Timeline panel to see all layers. For now, the movie clip consists of only one frame.

5 Click the Back button (⇦) at the left of the Edit bar to exit symbol-editing mode.

6 Choose File > Save As. In the Save As dialog box, navigate to your Lesson06 folder, choose Flash CS5 Document (*.fla) from the Save As Type/Format menu, type **Simple.fla** in the File Name/Save As text box, and then click Save.

Nesting movie clips inside movie clips

▶ **Tip:** A Flash document can have multiple independent scenes (Insert > Scene), which are played in sequence when exported as a movie. You can select which scene you're working on from the Edit Scene menu button located near the right end of the Edit bar.

As you have seen, the entire home page is contained inside a single movie clip placed on the Stage in Scene 1, Layer 1, frame 1. You'll now explore what's placed inside the first frame of the more complex document index.fla.

1 To view the document index.fla, click the index.fla tab at the top of the document window or choose Window > 1 index.fla.

2 In the Timeline, note the two layers. The layer *MAIN AS3* contains Action-Script code (indicated by the "a" in the upper half of the frame) but no other content (indicated by the hollow circle in the lower half of the frame). The layer *content* contains content (indicated by the filled circle in the lower half of the frame).

▶ **Tip:** ActionScript code, or actions, can be attached to any frame. It is considered best practice to place actions in their own layer at the top of the Timeline.

You will be looking at the ActionScript code in the top layer later. For now you're only interested in the content placed in the second layer.

3 Click to select the first frame in the layer content. Choose Edit > Select All and View > Magnification > Show All. You'll see three cars placed offstage to the left, but the Stage is black. In the Properties panel, note that the currently selected object is a movie clip named site (as in website).

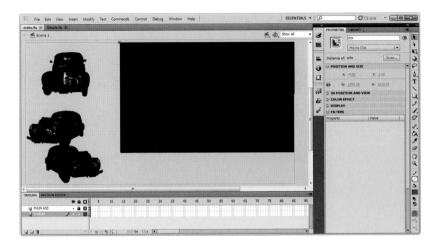

4 Choose Edit > Edit Selected to enter symbol-editing mode. Note the path to the symbol currently being edited—the movie clip site in Scene 1—in the Edit bar at the top of the document. In the Timeline you'll see four layers named nav, logo, home, and container. Only the first frame of each layer is filled with content.

● **Note:** When the movie clip site is played, it will trigger the objects placed on these four layers to be displayed, or played, concurrently.

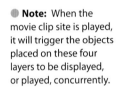

5 Click to select the first frame in the layer *home*. Choose Edit > Edit In Place. Note the path to the symbol currently being edited—the movie clip home inside the movie clip site in Scene 1—in the Edit bar at the top of the document.

6 Choose View > Magnification > Show All and Edit > Deselect All.

7 Use the scroll bar at the right side of the Timeline to scroll up and down, and review the many layers contained in the movie clip home. Use the scroll bar at the bottom of the Timeline to scroll sidewise and review the change of content in frames 1 through 225.

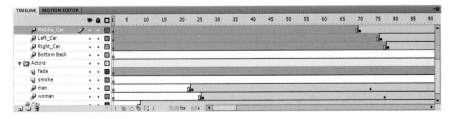

8 When you're done, scroll all the way to the left to return to frame 1.

Note: Dragging the current-time indicator in the Timeline to preview an animation is referred to as *scrubbing*.

9 Drag the current-time indicator at the top of the Timeline toward the right and watch the animation of the objects in the main document window.

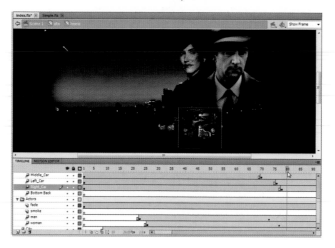

▶ **Tip:** You can also reach a specific frame by clicking the current frame readout (the first blue number at the bottom of the Timeline) and entering the frame number you want.

10 Stop dragging when you reach frame 191. Use the scroll bar at the right side of the Timeline to scroll all the way up, if necessary, to see the layer actions. Click to select frame 191 in the layer actions. This frame contains ActionScript code.

11 Choose Window > Actions to open the Actions panel. The ActionScript code consists of a single line:

```
stop();
```

causing the playback of the movie to stop here. Playback will only continue—here or elsewhere—when triggered by an event such as a user interaction.

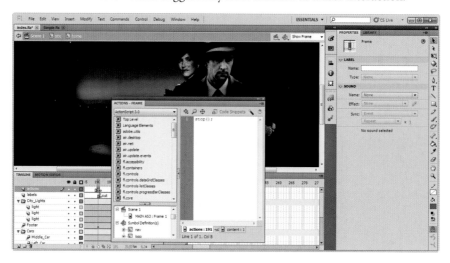

12 Close the Actions panel and choose Edit > Edit Document to exit symbol-editing mode.

In case you were wondering: You will not find the other pages of the site, such as the actors page, placed in any of the frames of the document. These pages are located as individual movie clips inside the folder *swf* inside the folder *Double Identity*. The movie clips are loaded dynamically into the layer *container*, triggered by a menu selection. To be precise, the buttons of the navigation bar react to mouse events (implemented as ActionScript code) and, when clicked, trigger the loading of the corresponding page.

▶ **Tip:** You can create a new movie clip symbol from an animation you've created on the Stage. See "Convert Animation On The Stage Into A Movie Clip Symbol" in Flash Help.

Working with timelines

You will now create an animation of the home page similar to the one you've just seen in the complex document.

1 Click the Simple.fla tab at the top of the document window.

2 In the Timeline, click to select the first frame in Layer 1. Right-click/Control-click the image in the document window and choose Edit In Place. Note the path to the symbol currently being edited—the movie clip home in Scene 1—in the Edit bar at the top of the document.

3 In the Timeline, hide the content of the layer folders Menu_Bar, Master Page Layer, and Logo by clicking in the column below the eye icon (👁) for each layer folder. For this lesson you'll animate only the images of the actors and the cars.

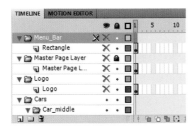

4 Try dragging the current-time indicator to the right; it will not move.

That's because the animation is currently only one frame long. Now you'll add frames to the Timeline to extend the duration of the animation.

5 In the Timeline, scroll down, if necessary, so you can see the layer Background inside the layer folder Background. Click to select the second frame in background image layer, and then choose Insert > Timeline > Frame.

The animation is now two frames long and the current-time indicator can be moved between the two frames. Your entire animation will be about 5 seconds long. At 12 frames per second that would be 60 frames. You'll extend the length of the Timeline span for the background image to 60 frames to remain visible throughout the entire animation.

6   In the Timeline, drag the second frame in the background image layer to the right. Release the pointer at frame 60. When you release the pointer, the background image duration will extend to 60 frames.

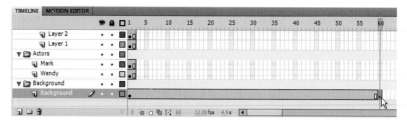

Creating motion tweens

▶ **Tip:** If the concept of frame animation is new to you, review the "Timelines And Animation" section in Flash Help.

● **Note:** Layers containing a tween have a tween icon next to their layer name in the Timeline.

You'll now create the animation for the image of the actor Mark. Using motion tweens enables you to define different properties of an object, such as position and opacity, in two separate frames. Flash then interpolates the property values of the frames in between to create the animation effect.

1   In the Timeline, click to select the first frame of the layer *Mark* inside the layer folder *Actors*, and then choose Insert > Motion Tween. The new motion tween is indicated by a span of frames with a blue background. The default length of the span is equal to one second in duration, or 12 frames in this 12 fps document.

2   Move the pointer over the right edge of the motion tween span. When the pointer changes to a horizontal double arrow (↔), drag the end of the span to the right. Release the pointer at the 60 frames mark.

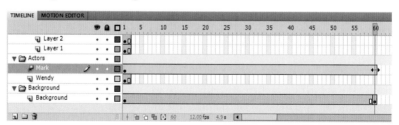

3 To have the image appear a short moment into the animation instead of already in frame 1, you'll now adjust the position of the first keyframe of the motion tween. Move the pointer over the left edge of the motion tween span. When the pointer changes to a horizontal double arrow (↔), drag the beginning of the span to the right. Release the pointer at the 9 frames mark. Drag the current-time indicator back and forth across the Timeline. Note that the image of the actor Mark is not visible on the Stage during frames 1 through 8 but is visible from frame 9 through frame 60.

● **Note:** If you position the pointer too far to the left, it will change to a horizontal double arrow with double bar (↔I↔), which you would use to adjust the column width in the Timeline panel.

To have the image fade in and slide into its final position, you'll create a property keyframe at the end of the fade, and then change the parameters of the keyframe at the beginning of the fade.

4 Position the current-time indicator at the 30 frames mark. Here is where the image should be fully visible and in its final position. Click to select the image of Mark on the Stage. In the Properties panel, choose Alpha from the Style menu in the Color Effect section. The Alpha value affects the opacity of the image. Leave the Alpha value at 100%, or fully opaque. By defining a color effect and then setting a property keyframe you can later create a color effect tween by changing the corresponding value in the first keyframe.

● **Note:** Pixels that are partly transparent in the original image remain partly transparent even with an Alpha value of 100%.

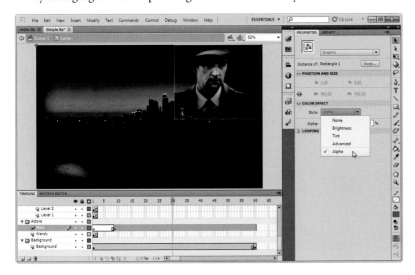

5 Choose Insert > Timeline > Keyframe. Property keyframes appear as small diamonds in the tween span.

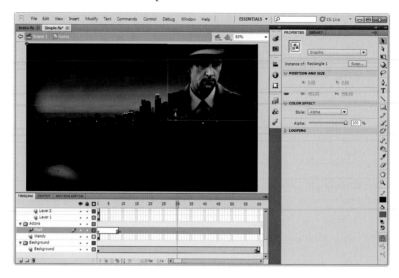

● **Note:** In Flash Professional CS5 and later, the concepts of a keyframe and a property keyframe are different. The term *keyframe* refers to a frame in the Timeline in which a symbol instance appears on the Stage for the first time. The separate term *property keyframe* refers to a value defined for a property at a specific time or frame in a motion tween.

6 Position the current-time indicator at the 9 frames mark, the first keyframe of the motion tween span. Here is where the image should be transparent and in its initial position. Click to select the image of Mark on the Stage.

7 In the Properties panel, set X: **-40** for the horizontal offset under Position And Size. Then set Alpha to **0**% under Color Effect to make the image fully transparent. Drag the current-time indicator in the Timeline from frame 8 to 30 to see the image fade in and slide to its final position. The animation for the image of the actor Mark is complete.

8   Repeat steps 1 through 7 for the image of the female actor Wendy, starting the animation two frames later and using +50 as the initial image offset.

9   Save your work, and then choose Control > Test Movie > In Flash Professional to review your animation in a preview window. The animation will loop, giving you a chance to review your tweens a couple of times. You'll also notice that the cars are appearing briefly each time the animation starts over again. When you're done reviewing, close the preview window. Next, you'll add a stop command at the end of the animation to keep it from looping and then deal with the car images.

Adding ActionScript commands

In this exercise you'll be adding a `stop();` command at the end of your animation to keep it from looping. You'll create an extra layer at the top of the Timeline where you should place all your ActionScript code so you can easily find them again when you return to your Flash project at a later time.

1   In the Timeline, use the scroll bar at the right side, if necessary, to scroll up so you can see the topmost layer folder Menu_Bar.

2   Click to select the layer folder Menu_Bar, and then choose Insert > Timeline > Layer. A new layer is created at the top of the Timeline.

3   Double-click the name of the new top layer and type **actions** as its new name. Press Enter (Return) to commit the name change.

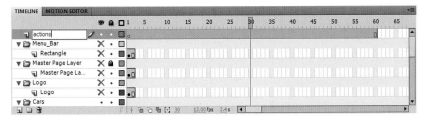

4   In the layer actions, click to select frame 60, the last frame of your animation.

5   Choose Insert > Timeline > Keyframe, and then open the Actions panel (Window > Actions).

6 In the Actions panel, click Code Snippets. In the Code Snippets panel, expand the Timeline Navigation folder and double-click Stop at this Frame.

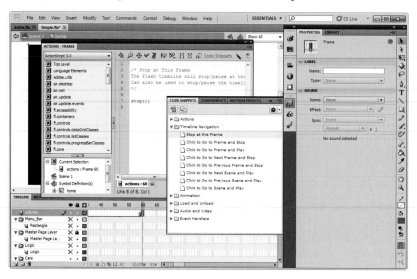

Tip: You can choose Window > Code Snippets to open the Code Snippets panel directly. After you double-click a code snippet, the Actions panel opens automatically to show you how the code was inserted.

The Code Snippets panel, new in Flash Professional CS5, lets you quickly inject prebuilt code into projects. This makes it easier to build projects without extensive coding experience. Because the code snippets contain comments, the purpose and use of each snippet is easier to understand.

If you're a programmer, using the prebuilt snippets speeds up the development process in several ways. You can add your own frequently used code to the Code Snippets panel and share code snippets with others to cut down on production time, and you don't have to worry about misspelling code.

7 Close the Actions panel.

8 In the Timeline, note the small "a" in the upper half of frame 60 in the layer actions, indicating that ActionScript code has been added to this frame.

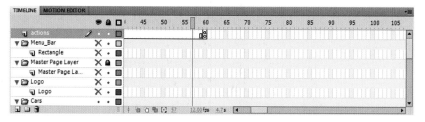

9 Choose Control > Test Movie > In Flash Professional. In the preview window, note that your animation only plays one time and then stops. Your first ActionScript script is working!

10 Close the preview window and save your work.

Creating symbols

To apply a tween to two or more objects as a group—such as the image of the car and the image of the headlights that should move in sync with the car—you need to first convert the group of objects to a symbol. The tween—such as a change in position or color effect—then applies to the symbol as a single object. The individual objects grouped within the symbol can in turn be as simple or as complex as you want them to be.

1 Click the Simple.fla tab and in the Timeline, drag the current-time indicator to frame 1. Using the Selection tool (↖), click either of the headlights of the car in the middle on the Stage. Hold down the Shift key, and then click to select the body of the car as well.

● **Note:** If you have difficulty selecting the headlights and car body, try Shift-selecting Layer 5 and Layer 7 (the same objects) in the Timeline instead.

2 Choose Edit > Copy.

3 Choose Insert > New Symbol. In the Create New Symbol dialog box, type **Car_middle_symbol** in the Name text box, choose Button from the Type menu, leave Library Root selected as Folder location, and then click OK.

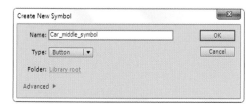

4 Choose Edit > Paste In Center.

5 Click the Back button (⇔) at the left of the Edit bar to exit symbol-editing mode for the Car_middle_symbol. Double-click the image on the Stage to enter symbol-editing mode for the home symbol.

6   In the Timeline, use the scroll bar at the right side to scroll down, if necessary, so you can see the two layers inside layer folder Car_middle inside the layer folder Cars. Select the layer Layer_7, the top layer inside the Car_middle layer folder, and then choose Insert > Timeline > Layer.

▶ **Tip:** Use the arrow keys to nudge the placed image into position.

7   From the Library panel (Window > Library) drag the Car_middle_symbol onto the Stage, aligning it with the other image of the car in the middle.

8   In the Timeline, select the two layers below the layer with the newly placed car symbol inside the layer folder Car_middle, and then click the Delete icon (🗑) in the lower-left corner of the Timeline panel to delete these two layers.

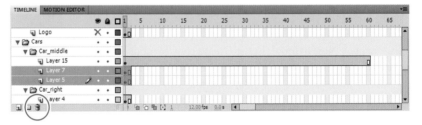

Animating symbols

You can now apply a motion tween to the Car_middle_symbol the same way you did for the images of the actors. This time you'll tween image size in addition to tweening the position and the opacity.

1   In the Timeline, click to select the first frame of the layer containing the Car_middle_symbol, and then choose Insert > Motion Tween.

2 Drag the first keyframe to frame 28. This is where the animation will start.

3 Position the current-time indicator at the 38 frames mark. Here is where the image should be fully visible, full size, and in its final position. Click to select the image of the car on the Stage. In the Properties panel under the Color Effect section, choose Alpha from the Style menu.

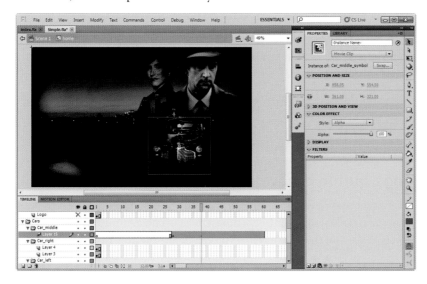

4 Choose Insert > Timeline > Keyframe.

5 Position the current-time indicator at the 28 frames mark, the first keyframe of the motion tween span. Here is where the image should be fully transparent, at reduced size, and in its initial position. Click to select the image of the car on the Stage.

6 In the Properties panel, set X: **800** and Y: **475** for the position under Position And Size. If the chain link icon appears broken (⛓), click it to change it to the locked chain icon (🔗) so the width and height will only change proportionally. Set W (Width) to **100**; H (Height) should change automatically to around 89 pixels. In the Color Effect section, set Alpha to **0**% to make the image fully transparent. Drag the current-time indicator in the Timeline from frame 28 to 38 to see the image fade in, become larger, and slide to its final position. The animation for the image of the Car_middle_symbol is complete.

▶ **Tip:** You can also position objects by dragging them in the document window.

7   Drag the current-time indicator to frame 1. Convert the left and right cars to button symbols and add a tween animation as you did in steps 1–6, using the following settings:

   • Start the left car's tween at frame 31. In the Properties panel name it **Car_left_symbol**, and then in the Position and Size section, set its X position to **700** and its Y position to **500**.

   • Start the right car's tween at frame 31. In the Properties panel name it **Car_right_symbol**, and then in the Position and Size section, set its X position to **1100** and its Y position to **500**.

   • Set W (Width) of both cars to **100**, and make both tweens 10 frames long.

8   Choose Control > Test Movie > In Flash Professional.

9   When you're done previewing, close the preview window and save your work.

Defining a button behavior

A button is a special type of four-frame movie clip. The first frame is displayed in the normal state, the second frame on a mouse-over event, and the third frame if the button is clicked. In the fourth frame you can define the area that should react to the mouse events—which could be smaller or larger than the button itself. The four frames are labeled Up, Over, Down, and Hit respectively.

1   Drag the current-time indicator to frame 42. Double-click the left car to enter symbol-editing mode for the Car_left_symbol.

2   In the Timeline, click to select the frame labeled Over in Layer 1.

3   Choose Insert > Timeline > Keyframe.

4   Choose Edit > Deselect All. Then click one of the headlights of the left car to select only the image of the two dimmed headlights. Choose Edit > Clear. The headlights of the left car are now turned on.

5 Drag the current-time indicator back and forth between the Up and Over frame to toggle the light.

6 Choose Edit > Edit Document to exit symbol-editing mode, and then choose Control > Test Movie > In Flash Professional.

7 Position the pointer over the left car. The headlights will turn on. Move the pointer away and the headlights will turn off again.

8 When you're done reviewing, close the preview window.

9 (Optional) Define a button behavior for the right car in the same manner.

10 Save your work.

For the car in the middle, you will define a rollover behavior shortly. But first, let's review how the rollover behavior is implemented in the complex home page.

Defining behaviors for movie clips

▶ **Tip:** In ActionScript 2.0 documents you can use the Behaviors panel to choose common events and corresponding actions from a predefined list. Flash then converts your specified behaviors to proper ActionScript code that you can review in the Actions panel.

When defining behaviors for buttons, the event handling happens behind the scenes. All you have to do is design the different states for your buttons. When dealing with movie clips, you'll need to write your own ActionScript code that triggers actions based on external events such as a mouse-over event.

1 To view the document index.fla, click the index.fla tab at the top of the document window or choose Window > 1 index.fla.

2 If the document is currently in symbol-editing mode, choose Edit > Edit Document.

3 In the Timeline, click the first frame in the layer *content,* and then choose Edit > Edit Selected.

4 In the Timeline, click the first frame in the layer *home,* and then choose Edit > Edit Selected.

5 Drag the current-time indicator to about frame 95 so you can see the middle car.

● **Note:** You can place multiple instances of the same symbol. You need to assign a unique name to each instance before you can access it in your ActionScript code.

6 Select the middle car on the Stage, and in the Properties panel note the name of this instance: *carMiddle.*

7 Double-click the carMiddle instance to enter symbol-editing mode.

8 In the Timeline, click the first frame in the layer actions. In the Actions panel (Window > Actions) note your old friend `stop();`. This command prevents the movie clip from playing past the first frame while waiting for an action.

9 Scrub the current-time indicator over frames 2 through 10. This is the animation that will play when the pointer is positioned over the car. Note the label `in` in frame 2 and the label `out` in frame 11 of the layer actions. Labels are used to address a specific point within an animation without relying on frame numbers. Frame numbers may change when frames are added or deleted to the Timeline, but labels move with the specific point on the Timeline.

10 Select frame 10 in the layer actions. Note the command `gotoAndPlay` (`'in'`); in the Actions panel. This causes the animation to loop between frames 1 and 10.

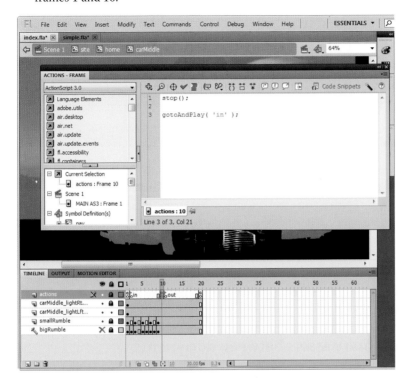

Triggering behaviors by events

The last piece to the puzzle is to see how the different behaviors are triggered by events. This, of course, is also done by ActionScript code.

1 Choose Edit > Edit Document to exit symbol-editing mode.

2 In the Timeline, click the first frame in the layer MAIN AS3.

3 In the Actions panel scroll down so you can see the lines 126 and 128. In line 126 you'll see the following command:

```
site.home.carMiddle.addEventListener(MouseEvent.ROLL_OVER,
onOverCarMiddle);
```

This command installs an event listener, a function that is executed when a specific event occurs, for the instance carMiddle on the home page. The event to listen for is a mouse rollover event and the function to be executed is called onOverCarMiddle. Note the similarity to defining a behavior in the Behaviors panel. The command in line 128 adds another event listener for a mouse roll-out event.

● **Note:** For a complete list of available ActionScript commands and their syntax, refer to the "ActionScript 3.0 (or 2.0) Language and Components Reference" in Flash Help.

4   Scroll down further so you can see lines 148 through 158 where the two functions onOverCarMiddle and onOutCarMiddle are defined.

The commands in lines 149, 150, and 151 are executed when the pointer is moved over the middle car. The command in line 149 positions the current-time indicator on the frame labeled in in the Timeline of the instance carMiddle, triggering the rumble animation. In lines 150 and 151 the two headlights are slowly turned on using a tween command to change the Alpha value of the two headlight images. (We combined the two headlight images to one image for the work on the simple page.) The function onOutCarMiddle, executed when the pointer is moved away from the middle car, stops the rumble animation and turns off the headlights again.

Copying library assets between documents

For the car in the middle, you still need to design the over state. You'll do this by copying library assets from one document to the other.

1   Close the Actions panel if it's getting in your way. From the Edit Symbols menu at the right end of the Edit bar at the top of the document choose Symbols > Cars > CarMiddle.

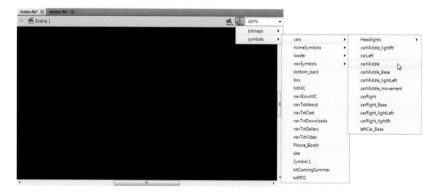

2 In the document window, click to select the headlight to your left. In the Properties panel, confirm that you've selected the movie clip with the instance name light2.

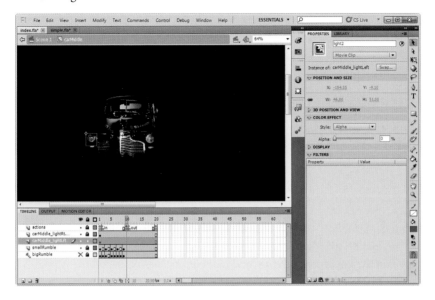

3 Choose Edit > Copy.

4 Switch to the document Simple.fla. From the Edit Symbols menu at the right end of the Edit bar choose Car_middle_symbol.

5 In the Timeline, click to select the frame Over (the second frame for a button symbol) in Layer 1.

6 Choose Insert > Timeline > Keyframe.

7 Choose Edit > Paste In Place.

8 Click to select the newly placed movie clip symbol in the document window. Under Color Effect in the Properties panel, set the Alpha value to **100**%. This will be the Over state appearance for the left headlight.

9   Switch back to the document index.fla. Try selecting the headlight to your right by clicking it. You'll notice that you can't select it the same way as the left headlight. You will first have to unlock the layer containing the right headlight in the Timeline. Locking layers enables you to avoid unwanted modifications. You can't select and thus copy or edit elements on locked layers.

10 In the Timeline, click the lock icon in the layer carMiddle_lightRgt.png. The lock icon disappears and the layer is unlocked.

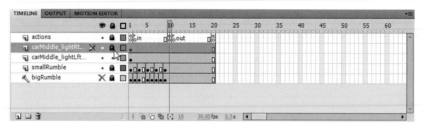

11 As you did in steps 3–7, copy the symbol light1 and paste it into place in the Car_middle_symbol of the Simple.fla document. Select the newly placed symbol in the document window, and in the Properties panel, set the Alpha value to **100**%.

12 Choose Edit > Edit Document to exit symbol-editing mode, and then choose Control > Test Movie > In Flash Professional. Move the pointer over all three cars to see the headlights go on and off.

13 When you're done reviewing, close the preview window and save your work.

You've finished the section of this lesson about creating a Flash document. In the next section you will learn to publish your Flash document for viewing in a web browser or as an AIR application.

Publishing a Flash document

Flash supports a variety of file formats to deliver your animation to an audience. For example, you can export your animation in SWF (Shockwave Flash, pronounced swiff) file format for playback using the Flash Player, create a complete web page for playback in a standard web browser, or create a stand-alone AIR application for playback on your desktop.

Exporting SWF (Shockwave Flash) files

If you intend to use your animation as content in another application, such as Dreamweaver, export the entire document as a SWF file.

1   Switch to the complex document index.fla.

2 Choose File > Export > Export Movie.

3 In the Export Movie dialog box, navigate to your Lesson06 folder, choose SWF Movie (*.swf) from the Save As Type/Format menu, type **Promo.swf** in the File Name/Save As text box, and then click Save.

● **Note:** You can specify publish settings for SWF files in the Flash tab of the Publish Settings dialog box (File > Publish Settings).

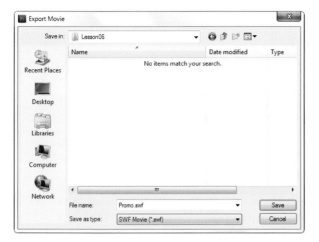

4 In Windows Explorer/the Finder, right-click/Control-click the file Promo.swf inside the Lesson06 folder and choose Open With > Adobe Flash Player from the context menu.

5 When you're done reviewing the document in the Flash player, close the file.

6 Launch Adobe Dreamweaver CS5, and in the Welcome screen, click HTML in the Create New section.

7 Choose File > Save As. In the Save As dialog box, navigate to the Lesson06 folder, type **index.htm** in the File Name/Save As text box, and then click Save.

8 Choose Insert > Media > SWF. In the Select File dialog box, navigate to the Lesson06 folder, select the file Promo.swf, and then click OK/Choose. (If you see an Object Tag Accessibility Attributes dialog box, click Cancel.)

9 Save the file, and then choose File > Preview In Browser > *[Web Browser Name]*. If you see an alert about copying dependent files, click OK. Depending on the security settings, you may need to allow blocked content before the website will open in your default web browser.

10 When you're done reviewing, close the web browser window and return to Dreamweaver.

Roundtrip editing between Dreamweaver and Flash

To make modifications to your website, you can open the SWF file in Flash from Dreamweaver. When you're done editing the site in Flash, the SWF is reexported and the changes are automatically reflected in Dreamweaver.

1 In Dreamweaver, select the placed SWF file in the Design view, and then click the Edit button in the Properties panel.

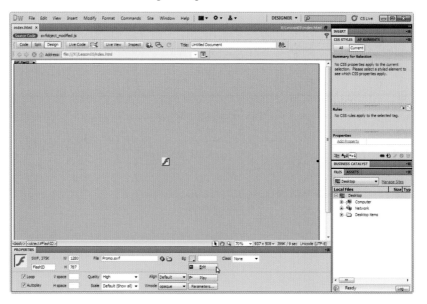

2   In the Locate FLA File dialog box, navigate to the Double Identity folder inside the Lesson06 folder, select the file index.fla, and then click Open.

3   Normally you would make changes at this point, but for this lesson you don't have to make any changes. You'll make the return trip to Dreamweaver from here. Click the Done button in the Edit bar above the document window.

The SWF file is reexported, and the content in the Dreamweaver document is automatically updated.

Publishing for playback in a web browser

Playing Flash content in a web browser requires an HTML document that selects the SWF file and specifies browser settings. The Publish command automatically generates this document from HTML parameters in a template document.

1   In Flash Professional, choose File > Publish Settings.

2 In the Publish Settings dialog box, select the Formats tab. If necessary, select the HTML option under Type, and then click the Select Publish Destination folder icon next to the HTML filename text box.

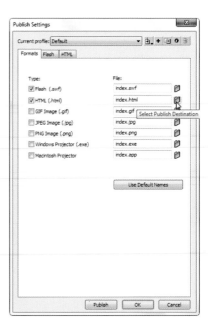

3 In the Set Publish Destination dialog box, navigate to your Lesson06 folder, leave the filename unchanged, and click Save.

▶ **Tip:** Your publish settings are saved with the document. Choose File > Publish to reexport the document with the same publish settings as last used.

4 In the Publish Settings dialog box, select the HTML tab. Choose Flash Only from the Template menu. From the Dimensions menu, choose Percent, and then type **80** percent in both the Width and Height text boxes. This will proportionally reduce the dimensions of the entire website, including all images, movies, and so forth. Leave the other settings unchanged, and then click Publish. A dialog box with a progress bar appears while Flash is creating the necessary files on your hard disk.

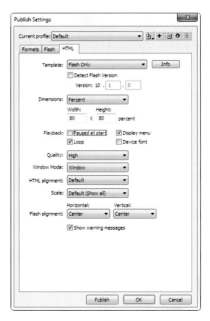

5 Wait until the publishing process has completed, and then click OK to close the Publish Settings dialog box.

6 In Windows Explorer/the Finder, double-click the file index.html inside your Lesson06 folder to open the exported website in your default web browser. If necessary, allow to show blocked content. Hover the pointer over the cars to confirm that your animation is still functioning—even at reduced size.

7 When you're done reviewing, close your web browser window and return to Flash.

Publishing for Adobe AIR

Adobe AIR is a cross-platform runtime environment that enables you to run AIR applications—such as Flash documents packaged as an AIR application—on your computer, providing all the convenience of a desktop application without the need for a web browser. The Adobe AIR runtime installer can be downloaded from the Adobe website at http://get.adobe.com/air.

To convert your document to an AIR application, do the following:

1 Choose File > Publish Settings.

2 In the Publish Settings dialog box, select the Formats tab. If necessary, select the Flash option under Type, and then click the Set Publish Destination folder icon next to the Flash Filename text box.

3 In the Set Publish Destination dialog box, navigate to your Lesson06 folder, leave the filename unchanged, and click Save.

4 In the Publish Settings dialog box, select the Flash tab. Choose Adobe AIR 2 from the Player menu. Leave the other settings unchanged, and then click Publish. A dialog box with a progress bar appears while Flash is creating the necessary files on your hard disk.

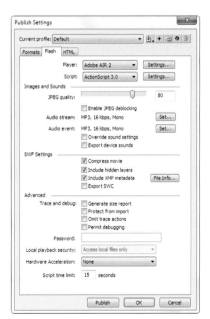

XFL: A more flexible Flash format

The Save As dialog box in Flash Professional CS5 contains a new option: Flash CS5 Uncompressed Document (*.xfl). What's the difference between this and the Flash CS5 Document (*.fla) option?

XFL is an XML-based implementation of the FLA file format, offering improved cross-product integration and workflow productivity. It isn't intended to create files for final distribution; instead, choose XFL to make a Flash project easier to work with across platforms or to exchange project data with other Adobe Creative Suite CS5 components such as Adobe InDesign.

This flexibility is possible because as XFL a project is uncompressed, and individual elements are more accessible. For example, an image that is currently used in a Flash project could be checked out of a source control system, updated, and checked back in. The next time you open the FLA project file, you would instantly see the updated image without having to manually import it into the project.

With better support for multiuser environments and cross-product compatibility, the XML-based format in Flash Professional offers the following benefits:

- The uncompressed format allows several users on a team to work on the same project simultaneously—no more having to split the project into multiple FLA files.

- Integration with source control systems is now possible because each team member can work on separate assets in the XFL package, eliminating the need to resolve differences.

- Mobile developers can work on the same files as other developers. (In the past, mobile content could not load other SWF files.)

Using XML-based FLA source files, Flash Professional CS5 provides a richer environment in which to exchange data with other key Adobe Creative Suite tools, including After Effects, InDesign, Illustrator, Adobe Encore, and Flash Catalyst.

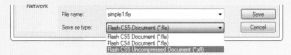

5   In the Signature tab of the Application & Installer Settings dialog box, select the option Use a code signing certificate, and then click the Create /New button.

6   In the Create Self-Signed Digital Certificate dialog box, type names of your choice in the Publisher Name, Organization Unit, and Organization Name text boxes (all text boxes must be completed). Choose your country's two-letter code from the Country menu. Type a password in the Password text box and again in the Confirm Password text box. Remember the password; you'll need it again in the next step. Choose your preferred level of encryption from the Type menu. Type a name for your certificate, click the Browse button, and select your Lesson06 folder as destination folder. Click OK to create your certificate, and close the Create Self-Signed Digital Certificate dialog box.

● **Note:** You can create an AIR Intermediate (AIR) application without a digital signature. A user is not able to install the application, however, until you add a digital signature.

7   In the Digital Signature dialog box, type the password in the Password text box.

8   Click OK to close the Digital Signature dialog box.

9   Click OK to close the dialog box that confirms that the AIR file has been created.

10 Click Publish.

11 Click OK to close the Publish Settings dialog box.

12 In Windows Explorer/the Finder, double-click the file index.air to start the installation of the AIR application to your computer. Click Install when asked for your confirmation to install the application. In the next screen, select the option Start Application After Installation, and then click Continue.

13 When the installation is complete, the website will start playing as a stand-alone application in its own document window.

14 When you're done reviewing, click the Close button to quit the AIR application.

Applying inverse kinematics animation

In addition to the animation capabilities you've already tried in this lesson, Flash Professional CS5 incorporates a dynamic physics engine into an advanced animation capability called inverse kinematics (IK). This capability is available in Flash Professional as the Spring property of the Bones element. Your animations will be more lifelike and less robotic.

For this lesson, you'll open a different file than the one you were using for the rest of the lesson.

1. In your Lesson06 folder, open the Spring folder, and then open the file Spring_start.fla.

2. Scrub the Timeline back and forth between frame 1 and frame 24 to show the simple animation of a map and several signs sliding onto the Stage.

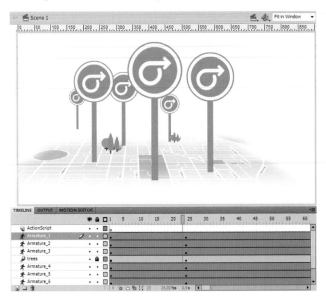

3. Move the current-time indicator to frame 24, and with the Selection tool, select the large sign in the center of the Stage. On the selected signpost you can see that an IK armature made up of two bones is applied to the sign.

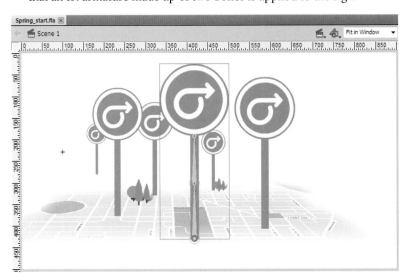

You create bones for a selected object by clicking the Bone tool (✐) where you want joints to be located.

4   With the Selection tool, select the top bone in the middle signpost; it will appear red. In the Spring section of the Properties panel, enter **20** for the Strength value, and then move the current-time indicator to frame 1 and press Enter (Return) to play the animation. The sign sways back and forth as the scene slides in.

The Strength and Damping options are new in Flash Professional CS5. Strength controls the intensity of the spring motion, whereas Damping controls how long it will take for the motion to gradually come to rest.

5   Select the top bone of the middle sign again, and then in the Properties panel enter **80** for the Strength value. Play the animation again and note how the sign sways much faster.

6   Select the top bone of the same sign again, and then in the Properties panel enter **50** for the Damping value. Play the animation from frame 1 and notice how the swaying motion gradually diminishes as the animation plays.

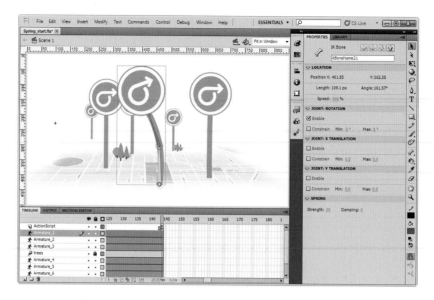

7   Select a different sign, select its top bone, and then enter **20** for the Strength
    value and **90** for the Damping value. Play the animation from frame 1 and note
    how the motion of the second sign diminishes sooner than the first sign.

Adjusting the Strength and Damping options in the Properties panel lets you customize the animation of individual objects.

Congratulations! You've finished this lesson about creating interactive documents
using Flash. As you've seen, Flash is a very powerful application, and we've barely
scratched the surface of all its possibilities. Nevertheless, you've created keyframe
animations and motion tweens, added rollover behavior for buttons, actually coded
in ActionScript, exported your creation as SWF file, learned about roundtrip editing with Dreamweaver, and converted your animation to an AIR application. In
addition, you explored the new Spring inverse kinematics feature that you can use
to enhance your animations.

Review questions

1   Describe the typical workflow for creating a Flash document.

2   What is a motion tween?

3   How do you add ActionScript code to your animation?

4   What is Adobe AIR?

5   What is the advantage of using the Spring option for the Bones tool when animating an object?

Review answers

1   To create an interactive document in Flash, you typically perform the following steps:

    • Plan the animations and how the user should interact with your document.

    • Create assets and import them into your Flash document.

    • Arrange the elements on the Stage and the Timeline to define when and how they appear in your document.

    • Add special effects and interactivity.

    • Test and publish your document.

2   Motion tweens are used to quickly create an animation effect. You only need to define different properties of an object, such as position and opacity, in two separate frames. To animate, Flash interpolates the property values of the frames in between.

3   Select any frame, and then open the Actions panel to enter the ActionScript code. For speed and convenience you can check to see if the code you want to add is already present in the Code Snippets panel, ready for you to drop in. It is considered best practice to place actions in their own layer at the top of the Timeline.

4   Adobe AIR is a cross-platform runtime environment that enables you to run AIR applications on your computer. If you package Flash documents as AIR applications, you can run them outside of a web browser. The Adobe AIR runtime installer can be downloaded from the Adobe website at http://get.adobe.com/air.

5   The Spring option for the Bones tool lets you create more realistic multiple-object interactions. You can produce more lifelike animations without having to animate proper physics manually.

7 DESIGNING FOR MOBILE DEVICES

Lesson Overview

In this lesson, you'll learn the following:

- Selecting a mobile device in Device Central

- Organizing mobile profiles

- Importing an image from Adobe Photoshop

- Optimizing content for mobile devices

- Previewing and testing artwork in Device Central

- Adjusting an image for mobile devices

- Creating snapshots

- Automating the testing process

- Publishing your work on Device Central

- Testing a mobile website

 You'll probably need between one and two hours to complete this lesson.

Streamline your mobile design workflow with tight integration between Device Central and other Creative Suite 5 Design Premium components. Device Central incorporates an extensive library of mobile device profiles, enabling you to quickly test the appearance and behavior of your mobile content in a simulated environment—right on your desktop!

Note: Before you start working on this lesson, make sure that you've installed the Creative Suite 5 Design Premium software on your computer, and that you have correctly copied the Lessons folder from the CD in the back of this book onto your computer's hard disk (see "Copying the Classroom in a Book files" on page 2).

Planning for a mobile device workflow

Now that you've created print and interactive PDF versions of a document, built a website, and added animation, you might want to use your design assets for a rapidly emerging type of output: content for mobile devices.

Mobile devices, such as cell phones, smart phones, PDAs (personal digital assistants), or gaming systems are like pocket-sized computers. Popular and widespread, these devices are small enough to be truly portable, yet powerful enough to readily access large amounts of information.

People can now view a wide variety of mobile web content on these devices, many of them paying additional fees for web browsing on their mobile telephones and hand-held computers. Developing successful content for delivery to these mobile devices requires that website designers work within special constraints. Text, images, and navigation all need to be optimized for small screens, and file sizes minimized to reduce download times. Adobe Device Central can facilitate the process of evaluating mobile design solutions for a wide variety of mobile devices, with emulation technology designed to simulate network performance of content on mobile devices in a realistic way.

To simulate real-life performance of your Flash Lite content, the Emulation workspace in Device Central helps you optimize your designs for the limitations of hardware and bandwidth. Device Central emulation gives you an idea of estimated download times and highlighting possible playback delays due to intensive interaction with a network server—enabling you to deliver a more satisfying end-user experience. You'll try emulation later in this lesson.

Typically, the process of evaluating your mobile content with Device Central follows a very simple workflow:

1 Locate a device profile in Device Central.

2 Preview and test your work in Device Central.

3 Make design adjustments in the original applications, such as Photoshop.

4 Publish your mobile content.

Using Device Central

In Device Central, you can preview and test your work as if you had hundreds of portable devices at hand. In the Emulate workspace, you can quickly view and assess a representation of the mobile content as it will appear on the selected device or devices. This method of testing is similar to the way you would preview website design in different target web browsers. The tight integration with other CS5 components streamlines the process: You can move smoothly between Device Central and Creative Suite components such as Fireworks, Photoshop, Illustrator, or Flash to adjust your designs before the final step of publishing the content to a handset.

Browsing the Device Library panel

In Device Central you can choose between profiles for hundreds of different brands and models of mobile devices, each containing the specifications and limitations for an individual handset.

1 Start Adobe Device Central CS5.

2 Under Device Profiles in the Welcome screen, click Browse Devices.

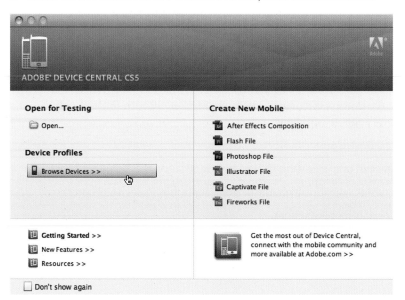

The Device Central main window opens. Notice the three panels: Test Devices, Device Library, and Library Filter. The Device Library panel lists all the currently available device profiles. If you're connected to the Internet, the first time you browse devices in Device Central it downloads the latest device profiles from the online device library maintained and updated by Adobe.

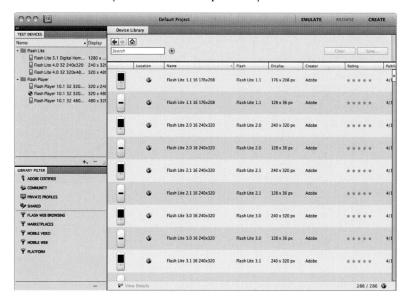

3   Before you begin working with Device Central, let's look briefly at some of the
    preference settings for Device Central. Choose Edit > Preferences (Windows)
    or Device Central > Preferences (Mac OS X).

By default, the Preferences dialog box opens to the General pane. The number you
see in the Default Phone ID text box is the International Mobile Equipment Identity
(IMEI) number of the device currently being emulated by Device Central. The
IMEI is a 15-digit number that uniquely identifies a device on the mobile phone
network—containing information about the origin, model, and serial number of the
device. Leave the default number unchanged for now; you'll choose a device later.

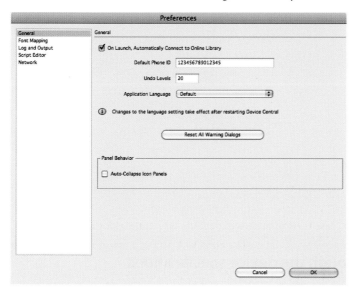

In the Application Language menu, you can change the language used in the Device
Central user interface. You must restart Device Central for this change to take effect.

4 Click Font Mapping. Here you can specify the fonts that will be used on your computer to emulate the actual fonts on the device.

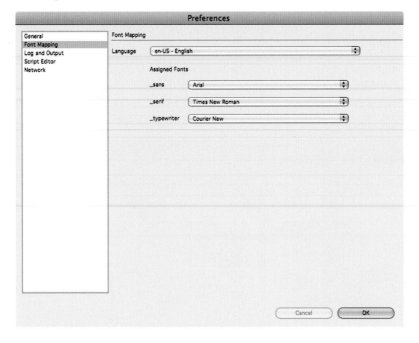

5 Click Cancel to close the Preference dialog box without making any changes.

Scanning through the device specifications

1 In the Test Devices panel, if necessary, click the triangle beside Flash Lite to expand the list of profiles. Select the Flash Lite folder to display the different models with their specifications on the right side of the main window.

2 Click in the empty area at the bottom of the Test Devices panel to deselect the Flash Lite folder.

You can sort the list by carrier, content type, display size, Flash version, manufacturer, or region. At one glance you are able to see the capabilities, constraints, and features of individual mobile devices. This is a very efficient way to research all the valuable pieces of information that can hugely increase your productivity in design development.

In the Device Library panel, when you see a globe icon (⊕) in the Location column it means the device profile is stored online. Once you've located the devices you want to test, you can drag them to the Test Devices panel. When you do this, the Location column icon for that device changes (⊕) to let you know that the device profile has been copied to your hard disk.

3   Select any device in the Flash Lite folder. To take a quick look at the key specifications of a selected device, you might need to make a panel or the window wider so that you see more details. As with other Creative Suite components, you can resize a panel by positioning the pointer at a panel edge until it changes to a double arrow that you can drag.

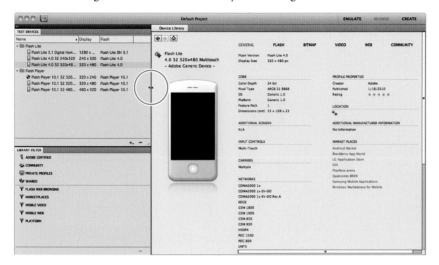

Note: When creating new documents, you can select Device Library only from your Test Devices panel. If the profiles that you want to use aren't already in your Test Devices panel, you'll first need to locate them in the online library and add them to your Test Devices panel.

4   Click in the empty area at the bottom of the Test Devices panel to deselect any devices. In the Device Library panel, click the plus sign next to the Search field. Click the Choose menu and choose Flash Version, choose Larger Than from the second menu, and choose Flash Lite 3.1 from the third menu.

5   Click the add button (⊕) to the right of the search criterion to add another. This time specify a color depth larger than 16 (bits per channel). Add one last criterion for a Display Size of Exactly **320**.

Tip: When you click the Save button in the Device Library panel, your search criteria are saved as a new filter in the Library Filter panel.

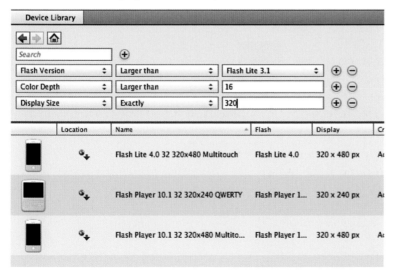

Tip: To view multiple devices simultaneously, Shift-click the device names for a consecutive selection, or Control-click / Command-click for a noncontiguous selection.

6   Double-click the first device on the list: Flash Lite 4.0 32 320x480 Multitouch. The Device Library panel displays detailed information for the selected device. Additional information is available in the Flash, Bitmap, Video, Web, and Community tabs.

You can drag a device to the Test Devices panel for easier access during a project. Doing this also saves a copy of the device profile from the online Device Library to your hard disk, so that you don't have to be online to use the profile.

7   Drag the device image to the empty area at the bottom of the Test Devices panel; it's added to the list.

8   With the newly added device selected, click the plus sign at the bottom of the Test Devices panel and choose Wrap into New Group. This puts the device into a new device group, which you may find convenient for organizing your devices. Click the group name, enter **My Devices**, and press Enter.

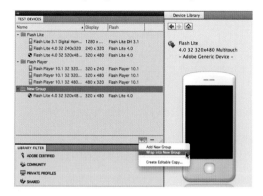 

Setting up to create mobile content

You can use Device Central to select a target profile before you even begin creating your mobile content in Creative Suite components such as Fireworks, Photoshop, Illustrator, or Flash so that you can start with a document that is already configured correctly. Take further advantage of the close integration of CS5 applications by previewing your design in Device Central and then quickly returning to the original editing program to fine-tune it.

1   In the Test Devices panel, select the profile you saved in the Test Devices panel, and click Create at the right side of the Application bar at the top of the window.

2   Click the large application icon and choose Fireworks. Notice the document size, 320 x 480 px, which will be used as the canvas size for your mobile design project in Fireworks.

3   Click the Create button at the bottom of the window. Device Central opens Fireworks and creates a new document using the specifications from the device profile.

▶ **Tip:** You can also drag an image from Adobe Bridge or the desktop and drop it into the Fireworks document window.

4   Choose File > Open, navigate to your Lesson07 folder, select the file localpicks_320x480.png, and then click Open. The image opens in Fireworks.

This is an image that was previously built in Fireworks for the same display size as the device you selected. However, it hasn't been tested on the device yet. You can use Device Central to preview the Fireworks document using the device profile you selected earlier.

Previewing and optimizing your mobile content

▶ **Tip:** If you can see the Optimize tab but it's collapsed, double-click the tab to expand the entire panel.

In most situations you'll need to make a compromise between image quality and file size to fit the specifications of mobile devices. Before making any adjustments in Fireworks, let's first preview the image for the selected profile in Device Central.

1   Choose Window > Optimize to open the Optimize panel.

2 In the Optimize panel, choose JPEG – Better Quality from the menu at the top of the panel, and then click the 2-Up button near the top-left corner of the window to compare the original with the web-optimized version.

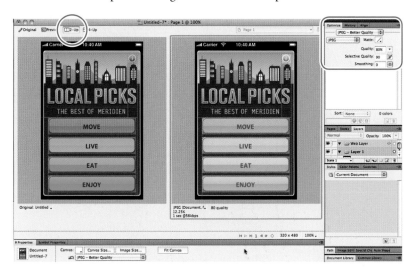

3 Choose File > Preview in Device Central.

Fireworks sends the image to Device Central and previews it using the device profile you started from. Notice that at the top-right corner of the window, Emulate Image is selected. You can always move among the Browse workspace for viewing and choosing device profiles, the Create workspace for starting a new document from the selected device profile, and the Emulate workspace for previewing your work on the selected device.

Emulate Image is designed to simulate the performance of various media types—such as Flash, bitmap, and video—on mobile devices in a realistic way. In the Content Type menu in the panel group on the right you can specify your mobile content as either a full-screen image, screen saver, or wallpaper. In the Display panel you can test how your image performs in different environments.

Note: If you are emulating performance for Flash content, make sure that the device you've specified supports the same Flash Lite version and content type. If your Flash SWF file requires Flash Lite version 2 and the emulated device supports only Flash Lite 1.1, the file will not appear in the Emulator view. You can sort devices by supported Flash Lite version to make sure that your mobile content is compatible.

4   In the Display panel, choose Indoor from the Reflections menu. In Emulate Image you'll see how your image might look on your mobile device by a window or under overhead lights.

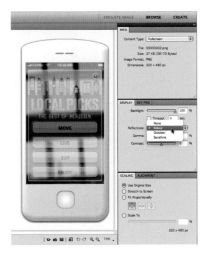

Creating images for mobile devices

You can use Device Central to create a new document based on a device profile, and Device Central can start that document in Photoshop, Illustrator, Flash, Fireworks, Captivate, or After Effects. Regardless of the component you use, your design has to take into account constraints such as screen size and color depth. In an environment of bandwidth and hardware limitations, the goal is to keep file sizes small.

To create files that are easy to edit and to keep file sizes down, simplify whenever possible. For Flash files, reducing the number of objects or making them less complex (fewer vector points) reduces greatly the amount of information needed to describe the artwork. For repeated objects, use symbols so that the artwork is defined only once instead of multiple times. For animations it's a good idea to limit the number of objects used and, where possible, to apply animations to groups of objects rather than to individual objects to avoid repetition of code. Additionally, compression can reduce file size dramatically. Therefore, you should keep in mind that depending on the content, using the SVGZ file format (scalable vector graphics file format compressed by gzip) could be a viable option.

Consider the following tips to create images that will display well on your targeted mobile device:

Work within the final size of the mobile device. Creating your graphics at the correct dimensions of your target device will help you achieve the best results. Use Device Central to start your document from the correct device profile (see "Setting up to create mobile content") to ensure that the file has the appropriate dimensions and color space for the target device. Scrolling is often impossible on mobile devices, so If content does not fit the screen, portions of it may not be accessible to viewers.

Reduce the number of colors. Consider using grayscale or reducing the number of colors as much as possible. Most of the common devices still support only 16-bit color (thousands), not 24- or 32-bit color (millions). Color effects such as gradients might be rendered as bands of solid color rather than smooth blends. WBMP (Wireless Application Protocol Bitmap Format), the standard format for optimizing images on mobile devices, supports only 1-bit color (black and white pixels) to keep the image size to a minimum. Applying the Sharpen filter to your images (possibly several times) increases the contrast, which can help reduce the number of colors.

5   Choose Outdoor and then Sunshine from the Reflections menu, and review the resultant effects on the image in the Emulate Image workspace. When you're done reviewing the simulation, select None from the Reflections menu.

Of course, an emulator cannot fully substitute for testing on real devices, but it can help you anticipate issues so that you can address them before you test on actual devices. You'll try more comprehensive testing methods later in this lesson.

6   Choose File > Return to Fireworks to quickly and easily switch back to Fireworks when you need to make changes based on the Device Central preview.

7   For this lesson, you're done working with this document, so choose File > Save As, navigate to your Lesson07 folder, name the file **mobile.png**, and click Save.

8   Choose File > Save As, locate your Lesson07 folder, name the Fireworks document Local Picks, click Save, and then exit Fireworks.

Viewing and refining Photoshop artwork

When you created a Fireworks document from Device Central, you may have noticed that you were able to choose from a number of Creative Suite 5 components. Some images are edited more effectively in Photoshop, so in this part of the lesson you'll do that. It's easy to jump quickly between Device Central and Photoshop to preview and refine your work.

1   Start Photoshop, choose File > Open, navigate to your Lesson07 folder, and double-click the document green_jacket.psd.

2   Choose File > Save for Web & Devices.

3   Choose the JPEG High preset from the menu at the top-right corner of the Save for Web & Devices dialog box.

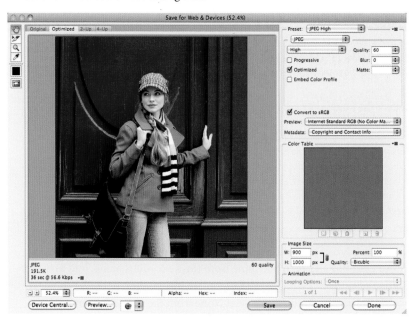

4 Click the Device Central button at the bottom-left corner of the dialog box. Device Central displays the image in the last device you selected. It's obvious that the image is too large; now you'll resize it properly in Photoshop.

5 Choose File > Return to Photoshop. You'll find yourself back in the Save for Web & Devices dialog box in Photoshop. Here, you can see why the image didn't fit: In the Image Size section, the image size is reported as 900 pixels wide by 1000 pixels tall—much larger than the 320 x 480 pixel size of the mobile device you're testing. Now you'll crop the image to the proper size.

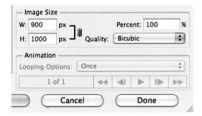

6 Click Done to exit the Save for Web & Devices dialog box.

7 Select the Crop tool. In the Options bar for the Crop tool, enter **320px** for Width and **480px** for Height. Leave Resolution blank.

8 Drag a crop rectangle that composes the image appropriately for the mobile device, and press Enter. Choose View > Actual Pixels to display the image at the size you entered in the Crop tool options earlier.

9 Choose File > Save for Web & Devices, and click the Device Central button to switch to Device Central and preview the image again in the Emulate Image workspace. This time the image size looks good on the device.

If you like, you can double-click other devices in the Test Devices panel to visualize the image on those devices. Of course, the size of this particular image will look correct only on devices with 320 x 480 pixel displays.

10 Choose File > Return to Photoshop. In the Save for Web & Devices dialog box, click Save.

11 In the Save Optimized As dialog box, navigate to your Lesson07 folder, select Images Only from the Save As Type/Format menu, name the file **green_jacket.jpg**, and then click Save.

Taking snapshots

It doesn't take much effort to change devices and to test your mobile content under different light conditions in the Emulator, but you might want others to see the results as well. Device Central CS5 enables you to take snapshots of your work at any point in the testing process and quickly share those snapshots with colleagues or clients.

1 Switch back to Device Central. With the image still emulated on the device, click the Take Snapshot button (📷) in the row of controls at the bottom of the Emulate Image workspace.

2 In the Display panel, choose Indoor from the Reflections menu, and then click the Take Snapshot button again.

3 Take a snapshot with each of the Outdoor and Sunshine Reflections options.

4 Click the Show Snapshots button (■) in the row of controls at the bottom of the Emulate Image workspace. The Log window opens and displays the snapshots (make sure the Snapshots button is selected at the top of the Log window). If needed, drag the Zoom slider to the left to fit the images on your monitor.

5 In the Log window, click the Export Snapshot Log As button (🖫) near the top-left corner of the Log window.

6 In the Export Snapshot Log dialog box, navigate to your Lesson07 folder, type **Device Snapshots** in the File Name/Save As text box, and then click Save.

7 Switch to Windows Explorer/the Finder and open your Lesson07 folder. Inside that folder, open the Device Snapshots folder that you just created on your hard disk. Double-click the index.html file to open it in your default web browser. When you're done reviewing the browser-based snapshot log, close the web browser window.

8   Return to Device Central, and close the Log window.

The ability to create snapshots and post them as web pages makes it easy to share your mobile device simulations with colleagues.

Publishing mobile content

When you've completed your reviews and finalized the mobile content, you can see your content on an actual handset display. Device Central offers different export options, all guided by a wizard for quick results, and avoids the need to use third-party tools.

To publish the image you just created, you can send it to a mobile device via Bluetooth or USB cable, upload it to a server via FTP, or copy it to your hard disk.

Provided you have a computer and mobile phone that are both Bluetooth-enabled, you can follow the instructions in the following exercise to export the image to your phone. Otherwise, reading through those steps will hopefully give you a good idea of the process.

1   In Device Central, choose File > New Project.

2   Navigate to your Lesson07 folder, name the project **Touchscreen.adcp**, and click Save.

3   Choose File > Open File. Navigate to your Lesson07 folder, select the file green_jacket.jpg you created earlier, and then click Open.

4   In Device Central, click Browse at the top of the window. In the Device Library panel, select a profile that matches your Bluetooth phone's characteristics, and then drag it onto the Test Devices panel.

About automated testing

Testing mobile content, especially games and animations, across a range of device profiles can be time consuming and complex. Device Central CS5 helps mobile developers to become more efficient by automating this task. You can record, save, edit, and share test sequences, including snapshots captured at specified frames. The Automated Testing panel enables you to record all interactions with the virtual phone as well as any changes made to the testing environment as a script, which you can modify with a JavaScript editor.

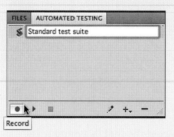

By pressing the Play button you can then run the script to batch process a selection of target handsets. Your content is loaded on the first mobile device, and the test script runs automatically. After the script has ended, Device Central switches to the next mobile device in your selection. When testing is complete, the Log window displays a detailed list of snapshots captured and errors detected, so that problems or bugs can be identified easily. Automating your testing can result in significant increases in productivity.

5 In the Tasks panel, click the New Task button (➕) and choose Send To Bluetooth Device from the menu.

Note: Bluetooth is a standard communications protocol primarily designed for low power consumption. It functions in short range (power-class-dependent: 1 meter, 10 meters, 100 meters). Bluetooth enables devices to communicate with each other when they are within range.

6 Switch on your Bluetooth-enabled mobile phone and make it discoverable. If necessary, refer to the instructions that came with your phone.

7 In the New Task: Send to Bluetooth Device dialog box, click Search, which will prompt Device Central to look for your mobile device.

8 Once your phone has been found, click Add, select the file green_jacket.jpg, and click OK. Then click Save to close the New Task: Send to Bluetooth Device dialog box.

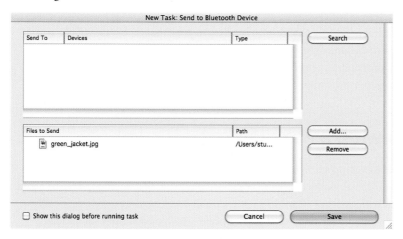

9 In the Tasks panel, click the Run Task button.

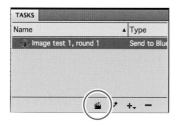

10 Under Send To in the Run Task: New Task dialog box, make sure that the check box next to your device is enabled and that the file green_jacket.jpg is listed under Files To Send, and then click the Save & Run button.

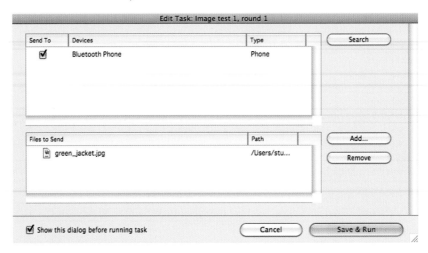

Device Central processes the file and sends it to your mobile phone, where you'll receive a notification of the transfer. Once the image is received by your phone, refer to the instructions that came with your phone to simply view the image or to install it as your new wallpaper or background image.

Previewing a mobile Flash Lite website

In addition to testing static images such as the wallpaper image from the previous exercise, you can evaluate other mobile content as well. For the next exercise you'll work again with imagery from the movie Double Identity: a website—especially designed for mobile devices—with background information about the movie.

1 In the Test Devices panel, double-click the profile Flash Lite 4.0 32 240x320.

2 In Device Central, choose File > Open Project.

3 Navigate to your Lesson07 folder. Open the folder Movie Promo and within that folder open the file MobileFilmSite.adcp, then click the Emulate workspace at the top-right corner of the window. The content of the project will be displayed in the Files panel.

4 In the Files panel of the Project window, double-click the file index.swf. Device Central displays the intro animation of the Double Identity home page.

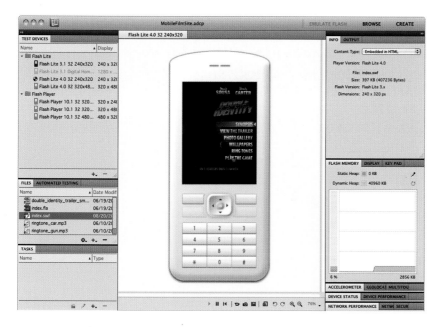

5   To move up and down the menu on the home page, click the navigation keys displayed below the virtual phone's screen. Alternatively, you can use the arrow keys on your keyboard or the navigation controls displayed in the Key Pad panel.

▶ **Tip:** Device Central CS5 emulates more than just the keypad. You can emulate the geolocation, accelerometer, and multitouch features of supported mobile devices.

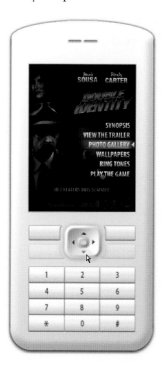

6   Now see how the movie trailer plays back on the phone. Select the View the Trailer menu item, and then click the virtual device's Select button or press Enter on your keyboard. The trailer plays on the screen of the device in the Emulate Flash workspace. To control playback of the video, click a button on the phone below the respective option displayed near the lower edge of the phone screen.

7   Select Back to return to the home page.

As you did previously in this lesson, you could test how the movie might look under different lighting conditions by choosing a setting from the Reflections menu in the Display panel.

8   Once you've explored this mobile website, you can quit Device Central.

Congratulations, you've finished this lesson about designing for mobile devices! You've learned a lot about Device Central's vast library of online profiles, as well as how to test different content from wallpapers to websites.

Review questions

1 What's the difference between the Test Devices panel and Device Library in Device Central?

2 How would you create new mobile content from within Device Central?

3 What is the Emulate workspace?

4 How can you quickly share your test results with others?

Review answers

1 The Test Devices panel offers Device Library that you've specifically added to your local computer. These profiles are available to you whether you have an Internet connection or not. The Device Library provides access to the Adobe online library of device profiles. These profiles are dynamically updated to ensure that each time you start Device Central, you will have access to the latest, most accurate information. Double-clicking any device profile in the online library will add that profile to your Test Devices panel.

2 With a device profile selected in Device Central, click Create at the top of the window, click the large application icon, and choose from the Creative Suite components listed in the menu that appears. Depending on your target profile, Device Central determines the document size to propose for the file you want to create and displays a picture and a matching size preset of the selected device(s) in the Create workspace. Click the Create button at the bottom of the window, and Device Central CS5 opens a new blank document in the CS5 component you chose.

3 The Emulate workspace in Device Central is designed to simulate network performance of content on mobile devices in a realistic way. A number of collapsible panels for testing and performance tuning appear in the Emulate workspace. Each panel has options for different media types, such as Flash, bitmap, and video, and offers options that apply to each type of content.

4 In Device Central CS5 you can take snapshots of your content at any time throughout your testing routine. Those snapshots will be collected together with the relevant device in the Snapshots tab in the Log window. You can easily share those results by exporting them from Device Central as HTML pages. You can send the HTML pages to your clients or colleagues, who can view them conveniently in a web browser.

8 SUBMITTING WORK FOR A PDF REVIEW

Lesson Overview

In this lesson you'll be introduced to the different types of PDF review and learn the techniques you'll need to take advantage of the exciting collaborative features in Acrobat and CS5:

- Attaching a PDF for e-mail-based review

- Adding and replying to comments

- Customizing the appearance of your notes

- Marking up a document

- Collaborating in online meetings

- Initiating a server-based shared review

- Tracking and managing PDF reviews

- Protecting your work

You'll probably need between one and two hours to complete this lesson.

Whether you want to get input on a spreadsheet or to collaborate on a design project, or you just need a project approved, Acrobat facilitates a range of review workflows. You can set up a review to suit your needs and have Acrobat keep track of comments, send notifications, and more. You can also collaborate live in online meetings—all in secure settings.

Introducing the different types of review

When it's time to present and share your work, Acrobat delivers many features to facilitate the review process. As you experienced in Lesson 1, you can also demonstrate and review your work live, directly from other CS5 applications such as Adobe Illustrator via the Share My Screen feature. You have a choice between different types of review—and for each of them there's a wizard to guide you step by step through the process.

● **Note:** Before you start working on this lesson, make sure that you've installed the Creative Suite 5 Design Premium software on your computer, and that you have correctly copied the Lessons folder from the disc in the back of this book onto your computer's hard disk (see "Copying the Classroom in a Book files" on page 2).

The e-mail-based review

An e-mail-based review is an excellent option when reviewers do not have access to a remote server or when it's unnecessary to interact with each other directly or in real time. Reviewers in an e-mail-based review have the opportunity to interact by replying to each other's comments once the initiator of the review has merged them. Later in this lesson you'll add and reply to comments in an e-mail-based review.

● **Note:** Only users of Adobe Acrobat Pro can initiate a document review and invite users of Adobe Reader to participate.

To start this review, the initiator sends an e-mail invitation to review the PDF file by choosing Comments > Attach for Email Review. The e-mailed PDF file includes comment and markup tools for the addressees to state their opinions. The Review Tracker enables the initiator to automatically merge those reviewers' comments into the master copy when monitoring them. You'll be guided through this process later on in this lesson.

The shared review

The highly collaborative nature of the shared review makes it the perfect solution for a group of people with common access to a centralized server. A shared review allows reviewers to read and reply to the comments of other participants rather than only being able to do so through the initiator.

When you initiate a shared review, you post a PDF file by choosing Comments > Send for Shared Review. The review can be hosted online in two ways: On Acrobat.com, or by specifying your own server location (a network folder, a Windows server running Microsoft SharePoint Services, or a web server folder). The reviewers receive an e-mail message with a link to the review location online. When they click the link, they can review the document in their web browser (if the PDF plug-in is installed) or they can download the PDF file and review the document within Acrobat. Reviewers can see the comments that other reviewers have made.

The Review Tracker in Acrobat facilitates the entire review process: Not only will the comments be merged and collected, but you can also invite additional reviewers as well as send e-mail reminders to participants.

The online, real-time review

There's no better way to show and tell than sharing your work online and live via your desktop. Adobe ConnectNow, a personal web-conference tool, enables you to conduct real-time meetings on your desktop. From Acrobat 9 Pro, you can create your own user account on Acrobat.com. You can upload and share most document types—or your entire desktop—in online meetings. This option becomes especially interesting when you want to share files in formats other than PDF or when you want to demonstrate an action within an application. A real-time online review can save so much time in collaborative discussions—not to mention the reduced travel costs!

Participants join the meeting by logging in to a web-based meeting space from their own computers, so obviously they require an Internet connection. In a ConnectNow online meeting, you can share just a document or your entire desktop, use live chat, share online whiteboards, and take advantage of many other collaborative features.

● **Note:** As an initiator of an e-mail-based review you cannot send an e-mail to yourself—unless you have two separate e-mail addresses.

Collaborating in an e-mail-based review

For the purposes of this lesson, where you'll be exchanging comments regarding the magazine cover you designed in Lesson 2, the process of conducting the review will be simplified. You may not have access to a shared server or a partner to participate in the review, but you can still get to know the relevant features in Acrobat and the interface and tools you'll use to collaborate in a review.

Following are the steps of this hypothetical review:

1 You initiate the review by using Acrobat to open a PDF file from your Lessons folder, and using an e-mail-based review to send the PDF file to your selected reviewers as an e-mail attachment.

2 You can review this PDF attachment, adding your remarks using the comment and markup tools in Acrobat or the free Adobe Reader.

3 Use the Review Tracker to monitor the comments that each reviewer has added to the PDF file.

Viewing comments

Your task is to review a magazine cover—evidently not sent as an e-mail attachment but as a PDF file in your Lessons folder—and add your comments using the comment tools in Acrobat. First, you'll want to view and assess the comments of other reviewers.

1   If you haven't already done so, launch Adobe Bridge.

2   In Bridge, navigate to your Lesson08 folder and double-click the file Local_Magazine_start_cover.pdf to open it in Acrobat 9 Pro.

3   If the Comment & Markup Toolbar is not already open, click the Comment button ( ) in the menu bar and choose Show Comment & Markup Toolbar.

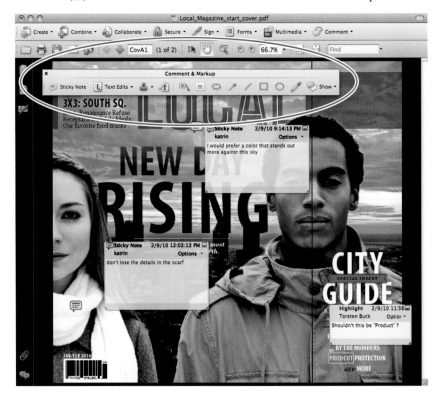

When reviewing a document, there are different ways to mark up and comment. In our example comments are made as sticky notes. Any comments added to a file being reviewed are recorded in the Comments List, which is located on the bottom of the document pane.

Attaching a file for an e-mail-based review

For an e-mail-based review, you can send out a tracked copy of a PDF, which makes it easy to collect and manage all the responses. You can explore this option provided you have an Internet connection, an e-mail address, and a colleague to work with.

1   In Acrobat, open the PDF file you want to send for review.

2   Choose Comments > Attach for Email Review. If this is the first time you've used this feature, the Identity Setup dialog box appears. You'll need to enter your information before proceeding.

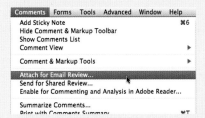

3   The Attach for Email Review command opens a wizard to guide you through the process of attaching a PDF file and specifying a master copy. All comments from the reviewers will be merged into this file.

4   Enter the e-mail addresses of the reviewers. To enter addresses faster, click Address Book to select addresses from the address book of the default e-mail application on your system.

5   Click Next. You can preview and edit the Subject and the Message of the e-mail that will be sent to the recipients.

6   Click Send Invitation. A copy of the PDF is sent to the reviewers as an attachment. It may be opened in your e-mail program and you may need to send it manually from there.

When this PDF attachment is opened, it presents with comment tools and instructions.

Whenever you receive comments to the review you initiated, the Merge Comments dialog box will appear. You can then merge the comments into the master PDF so that they're all in one location.

Note: In Reader, comment tools are available only for PDF files that have commenting enabled. PDF files in a review workflow typically include commenting rights.

4   To see the list of comments, click the Comments button (📑) at the bottom of the navigation pane.

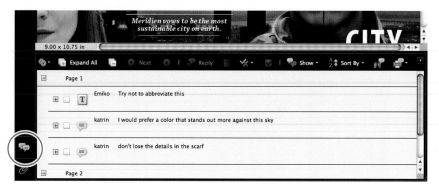

By default, comments are sorted according to the page on which they appear. However, you can change that order to sort the comments by author, type, date, color, or checked status.

▶ **Tip:** To view only the comments of a particular reviewer, click the Show button on the Comments List toolbar, choose Show by Reviewer, and then select the name of the reviewer. All comments from other reviewers will be hidden. To display all of the comments again, choose Show by Reviewer > All Reviewers.

5   Change the sorting order by clicking the Sort By button in the Comments List toolbar and choosing Author. An Acrobat dialog box appears with some tips. Click OK.

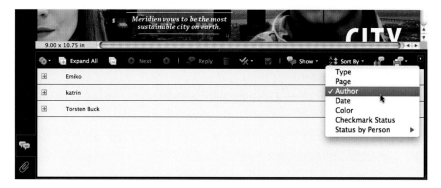

6   Click the plus sign next to an author's name to expand that reviewer's comments.

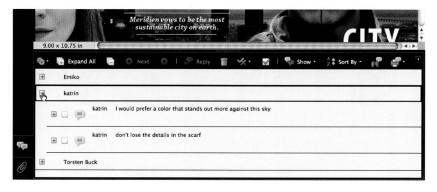

7   Click the yellow sticky note under the name Katrin. Acrobat will highlight the corresponding sticky note on the document with a halo.

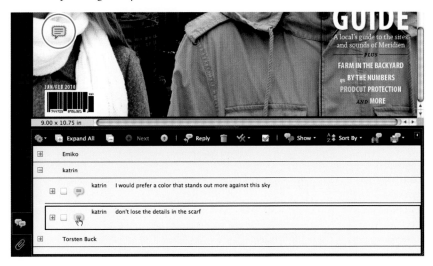

8   Move the pointer over the highlighted yellow sticky note on the magazine cover. The text of the comment becomes visible.

9   Double-click the yellow sticky note icon to open the associated pop-up window, and then drag to position the pop-up window anywhere you want on the magazine cover.

Uploading a file for a live collaborative review

By using the Acrobat.com online service, you can communicate via live chat and review a PDF file live online with your colleagues.

1 In Acrobat, open the PDF file you want to send for review.

2 Choose File > Collaborate > Send & Collaborate Live.

3 Sign in to Acrobat.com with your Adobe ID (or click Create Adobe ID to make one), then click Next.

4 Preview and edit the recipients, Subject, and Message of the e-mail that will be sent to reviewers. Clicking the To and CC buttons lets you select addresses from the address book of the default e-mail application on your system.

5 Select the Store File on Acrobat.com and Send a Link to the Recipients checkbox to host your PDF file on Acrobat.com. This is useful when the PDF file is large because the e-mail doesn't need to include an attachment; instead the receipient gets a small email and a download link. If you prefer to send an attachment, leave the Store File on Acrobat.com and Send a Link to the Recipients checkbox deselected.

6 Click Send. When the PDF file is opened by you or any recipient, it displays the Collaborate Live panel which provides the opportunity to go online and start a live collaborative review immediately.

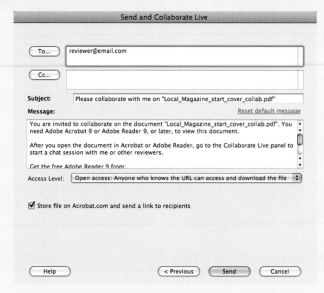

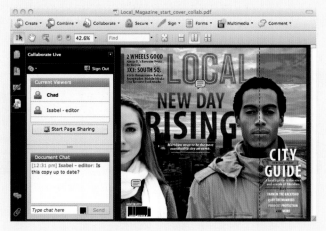

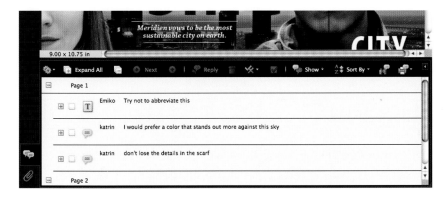

All comments can be moved around the page except text markups. You'll appreciate this when you receive documents for review that are cluttered with comments.

You can hide or show comments by filtering them based on the reviewer. When you summarize or print comments, you can specify whether hidden comments appear. Hiding a comment that has been replied to will hide the entire thread associated with that comment—that is, all the replies and discussion on the comment.

● **Note:** In an e-mail-based review, hidden comments aren't included when you send your comments to the initiator.

Replying to a comment

Now that you've seen the other comments and are part of the review, you'd probably like to put in your two cents worth, as well. Acrobat gives you a wide choice of comment and markup tools for giving feedback and communicating your ideas.

Not only can you type text comments into the familiar sticky notes, you can also add arrows and shapes, and draw freehand directly onto the file to illustrate your point or highlight parts of the text and add callouts. You can modify the appearance of your comments by changing the color of the sticky notes or the type style, which you'll be doing as part of the next exercise. An array of stamps helps you to efficiently comment and mark standard business documents, and you can also create and customize your own stamps. Provided you have the appropriate hardware and software installed, Acrobat even lets you add audio comments.

Next, you'll reply to one of those yellow sticky notes from this e-mail-based review.

1 With the Comments List still open in the navigation pane, select the comment from Katrin that says, "don't lose the details in the scarf."

2 Click the Set Status button on the Comments List toolbar and choose Review > Rejected.

The rejected status is indicated by a red cross below the comment in the list.

3 With Katrin's comment still selected, click the Reply button (🗨) in the Comments List toolbar.

4 A reply box opens where you can explain why you rejected the design. We wrote: **We checked the numbers and it also proofs properly. Thanks**.

5 Alternatively, you could also open a reply window by choosing Reply from the comment's Options menu.

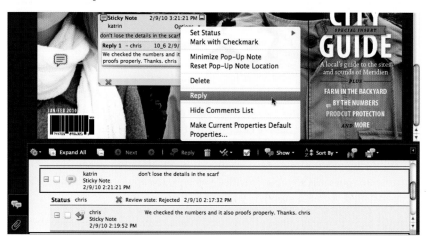

6 Close the sticky note by clicking the Close button on the upper-right side of the sticky note.

Customizing the appearance of your notes

Finally, you'll add your own comment—this time via the Comments menu—and then change the color of the sticky note to make your statement more prominent.

1 In the Comment & Markup Toolbar, select the Sticky Note tool. Click to add a new sticky note on the man's shoulder.

2 If the yellow sticky note isn't open, double-click to open it, and then type your comment. We wrote: **This jacket worked out well!**

3 Click the comment's Options menu and choose Properties.

Note: To delete a comment, Ctrl-click / right-click the sticky note and choose Delete.

4 In the Sticky Note Properties dialog box, click the Color swatch to open the color picker, choose a bright blue, and then click OK.

5 Now your note stands out among the others.

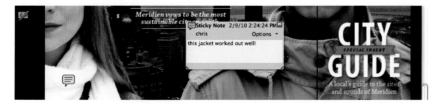

Marking up a document

As you may have noticed, the Comment & Markup Toolbar includes specialized tools for editing a document. You can use the Text Edits tool to insert or replace text, underline text, or cross it out to mark it for deletion. Your text edit comments do not alter the actual PDF file; they merely indicate where text should be inserted and which text should be deleted or replaced in the source file from which the PDF was created.

1 In the Comment & Markup Toolbar (note how it docks to the upper panel) select the Text Edits tool. If this is the first time you've used this tool, the Indicating Text Edits dialog box appears with tips for some standard text edits; once you've read them, you can click the Don't Show Again box, and then click OK.

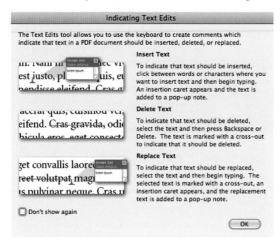

2 With the Text Edits tool still active, select the word DAY in the NEW DAY RISING headline. Click the triangle beside the Text Edits tool to open a menu of tool options and choose the Replace Selected Text tool.

Protecting your work

You can use passwords to restrict unauthorized users from opening, printing, or editing a PDF file. You can use a certificate to encrypt a PDF file so that only an approved list of users can open it. If you want to save security settings for later use, you can create a security policy to store your security settings.

By adding security to documents, you can limit viewing, editing, printing, and other options to specified users. You can choose if you prefer the users to have a password, a digital ID, or access to Adobe LiveCycle Rights Management.

Security methods

Acrobat provides a variety of security methods for specifying document encryption and permission settings. You can encrypt all or part of a document and limit user actions. For example, you can allow users to input only in form fields or prevent them from printing a PDF file.

Each security method offers a different set of benefits. However, they all allow you to specify encryption algorithms, choose the document components that you want to encrypt, and set different permissions for different users. Use the Document Properties dialog box to choose one of the following security methods:

- **Password security** provides a simple way to share documents among users when sharing passwords is possible or when backward compatibility is required. Password policies do not require you to specify document recipients.

- **Certificate security** provides a high level of security, eliminates the need for password sharing, and allows you to assign different permissions to different users. Also, you can verify and manage individual user identities.

- **Adobe LiveCycle Rights Management policies** are stored on a server, and users must have access to the server to use them. To create these policies, you specify the document recipients from a list on Adobe LiveCycle Rights Management.

For more information regarding security, refer to Acrobat Help.

3   With the letters still selected, type your replacement text (we wrote: DAWN). As you start typing, the pop-up note window should open if needed.

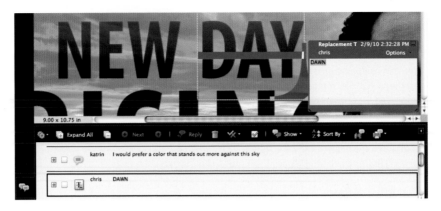

4   For the purpose of this exercise there is no need to save any changes to your review work—just close the Local_Magazine_start_cover.pdf file.

Tip: For major editing work, the specialized markup tools are faster, clearer, and easier to use than simply adding a sticky note and describing an edit.

Tools like the Highlight Text tool and the Underline Text tool can be used to add comments either on their own or in conjunction with notes. Acrobat provides you with a variety of options for text edits: You can highlight parts of the text and add a note, or cross out selected text by clicking the triangle beside the Text Edits tool to open a menu of tool options. Select the Replace Selected Text tool, and then enter your corrections in the associated pop-up note. You can also use the Cross-Out Text tool to quickly indicate text to be deleted, or even faster, simply click the Text Edits button, select the text, and press the Delete key.

Managing reviews

Note: RSS (Really Simple Syndication) is used to publish frequently updated content (e.g., news headlines, blog entries, or podcasts). The RSS format is compatible with XML and RDF formats.

In a managed review, a wizard will help you set up your review and invite the participants. The Tracker, as its name implies, helps you to keep track of the review. The Tracker lets you manage document reviews and enables you to distribute forms as well as administer RSS feeds (online subscriptions to updated content). No longer do you have to import comments, enable commenting for Reader users, or manually track reviewers' responses.

Even if you did not initiate a shared review but are merely a participant, published comments on your local hard drive are synchronized with the comments on the server. You are notified whenever new comments are published—even when the PDF file is closed, as synchronization continues.

Working with the Tracker

Because you might not be connected to the Internet or have e-mail access on your computer, let's just imagine for the purposes of this exercise that you did initiate the cover review—though your Tracker dialog box will look different from the illustration. Some of the settings for the Tracker can be specified in the Acrobat

Initiating a shared review from the Tracker

If you have an Internet connection, an e-mail account, and use Acrobat 9, you can explore initiating a shared review using the Tracker to help you manage the review.

1 In Acrobat, choose Comments > Track Reviews. A wizard will guide you through this process.

2 When the Tracker dialog box appears, click Create A Shared Review.

If this is the first time you've initiated a shared review, a dialog box will appear, asking you to create your own user account at Acrobat.com. This account can be set up from either Acrobat or Reader and enables you to upload and share large documents in most common formats, and also to share your desktop in online meetings.

If you are already participating in reviews using the Tracker, the Tracker dialog box displays more details about those reviews, as well as forms, server status messages, and RSS feeds.

Once the wizard has guided you through setting up the review, you can enter an e-mail list of reviewers and invite them to participate.

Preferences dialog box. To initiate a review yourself, look at Initiating a Shared Review later in this chapter to get started with the Tracker wizard.

1 In Acrobat, choose Comments > Track Reviews to open the Tracker dialog box. To open the Tracker in Reader, choose View > Tracker. In the left panel, we were able to select the Local_Magazine_start_cover.pdf under Reviews Sent, because we initiated that review.

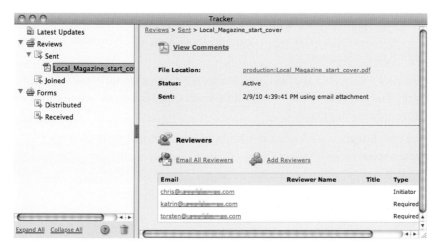

Note: In the Tracker, the Sent section lists only the PDF files in reviews you initiated.

About approval workflows

For some PDF reviews you only need to get a document approved, rather than collect a lot of comments. Acrobat enables you to send a PDF file as an e-mail attachment for others to approve—even in Chinese, Japanese, and Korean!

When participants open an approval request in Acrobat, they can approve the PDF by adding a digital identity stamp from the Stamps palette, which automatically appears when you open a document that's set up for an approval workflow.

They can send the PDF to others for approval via email or return the PDF to the initiator and other appropriate participants. The initiator can track progress by choosing to be notified each time the PDF is approved. The workflow ends when the last participant adds the final approval. If a PDF isn't approved, the approval workflow must be started again.

Since you are already an active reviewer, the left panel of the Tracker dialog box displays more details about the reviews, forms, server status messages, and RSS feeds—should you want to participate in those. The Latest Updates panel gives you a summary of all the latest changes to reviews in which you are a participant. You can turn Tracker notifications on or off in Acrobat and, for Windows only, in the system tray.

The right panel shows the review details for the item selected in the left panel—in our case the magazine cover review. Because published comments on your local hard drive are synchronized with the comments on the server, you'll be notified automatically when new comments are available.

To look at the comments from the Tracker, click View Comments to go straight to the sticky notes on the document in Acrobat's main window. At any time during a review the initiator can invite more reviewers by clicking Add Reviewers and entering their e-mail addresses.

2   Ctrl-click / right-click the file Local_Magazine_start_cover.pdf in the left panel of the Tracker, and choose E-mail All Reviewers. This is a quick way to contact all the other reviewers.

3   You can close the e-mail window when it appears, because there is no need to write a message.

4   As the initiator you can discontinue a shared review by Ctrl-clicking / right-clicking the PDF file and choosing End Review.

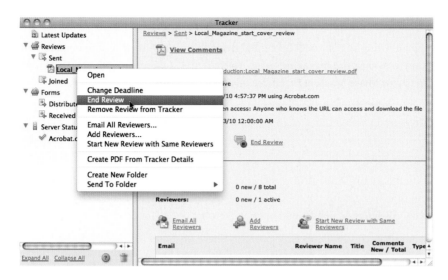

Once a review has ended, participants cannot publish comments to the server. You can restart the review by extending the deadline.

Collaborating in online meetings

There may be times when you want to hold an online meeting that involves more than one document or application. In these cases you can't use the shared review described earlier in the chapter because that's based on a single document. Instead you can use Adobe ConnectNow, a personal web-conference tool that you can use to conduct real-time meetings—sharing a document or your entire desktop, and using live chat, online whiteboards, and other collaborative features. As an attendee you join the meeting by signing in to an online meeting space using a web browser on your computer.

The great thing about this kind of online meeting is that everybody has the same view—which is set up by the person conducting the meeting. As the initiator, you have complete control of what your clients or colleagues are seeing while you walk them through the project.

An online meeting can be highly productive when it comes to sharing ideas, discussing detailed issues, and collaborating on a project. As a matter of fact, ConnectNow helped a lot in the writing of this book because the various Adobe product teams were able to demonstrate some of the new features of the Creative Suite live to colleagues who were geographically dispersed. Version control, platform compatibility, and even having the same programs installed are no longer an issue. You can enable video conferencing, send instant messages, and even permit another participant to take control of the desktop. Interaction takes place in real time, which makes the meeting more personal and more fun.

▶ **Tip:** Although Acrobat is the example used in this chapter, ConnectNow shared meetings aren't limited to Acrobat. You can use ConnectNow to share any file or application on your computer.

Note: CS Live online services are complimentary for a limited time. See the sidebar "Accelerate your workflow with Adobe CS Live" on page 25 for details and limitations related to all Adobe online services.

Working with Share My Screen

On the following pages, you'll be guided through the process of setting up an online meeting to discuss the magazine cover. To share this document from your desktop, you'll use the Share My Screen feature from within Acrobat.

You'll be guided through the process of setting up your online meeting. However, you do need an active Internet connection to work with Share My Screen. If you're not connected to the Internet, you can still follow some of the steps in this exercise and simply skim others.

1 Switch back to Adobe Bridge, select your Lessons folder in the Favorites panel, and then navigate to the Lesson08 folder. Double-click the file Local_Magazine_start_cover.pdf, which should open in Acrobat.

Tip: In CS5 components other than Acrobat that support Share My Screen, holding down the CS Live button at the right end of the Application Bar is another place to choose Share My Screen, and also a way to use other CS Live online services*.

2 In Acrobat, choose File > Collaborate > Share My Screen. Enter the e-mail address and password that you use as your Adobe ID, and click Sign In.

If you don't already have an Adobe ID, click Create Adobe ID and when you're done with that, return to Step 2.

It will take a moment for the server to sign you in; then the Welcome to Connect Now Meeting Room dialog appears offering you two choices:

- Customize Your Meeting URL. The end of the URL is your name by default, but you can change it to something that better describes the nature of the meeting, or to a word or phrase that's shorter or easier to remember.

- Send E-Mail Invitation Now. This option opens the default e-mail client on your system with a message that contains the URL for your meeting. You'll have an opportunity to edit the message before you send it.

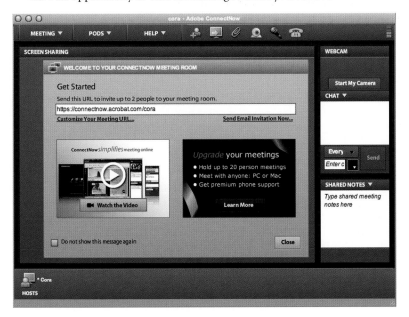

3   If there's someone who can join you for this exercise and they have Acrobat 9 or Acrobat Reader 9 installed, you can click Send E-Mail Invitation Now, and they can be your attendee. Or you can make a note of the URL and click Close.

If you have access to another networked computer, you can enter the URL into a web browser on that computer to see how Share My Screen looks from the point of view of an attendee. Attendees don't need an Adobe ID; they can sign in as a guest and the meeting host can decide whether to let them in.

4   Click Share My Computer Screen to start the meeting. You may be asked to approve the installation of the Adobe Connect. Now add-in for your web browser; click Yes.

You'll be asked what you want to share—your entire computer desktop, individual windows, or a specific application. When you've got windows open with information you don't want the meeting participants to see, it's a good idea to restrict what you display to others, limiting screen sharing to one application or even just one window.

Note: On Mac OS X, at this step ConnectNow may open the Universal Access system preferences pane and display a message about assistive devices. If this happens, turn on the Enable Access for Assistive Devices option and return to your web browser.

Tip: To make your messages stand out, you can customize your Chat pod by choosing fonts, sizes, colors, and emoticons.

5   Click Windows, then in the list select Local_Magazine_start_cover.pdf.

While the meeting is in progress, the ConnectNow screen sharing panel is displayed, giving you access to key meeting features and enabling you to share notes, send chat messages to one person or the whole group, use an online whiteboard to sketch ideas, activate a webcam, and even turn over the control of your desktop to another attendee, which can be very productive for collaborative work sessions and technical support. You can position the ConnectNow screen sharing panel wherever you want on your desktop.

6   The open Acrobat file on your desktop is now shared with the other participants. Notice the ConnectNow screen sharing panel where you can type chat messages to other attendees, and also control various meeting tools such as your webcam.

7   When an attendee wants to join the meeting, an alert will appear. Click Accept to admit that attendee to the meeting room. The attendee receives a note to let them know that the host has been notified of the attendee's presence.

The Chat window is useful for side discussions during the meeting, as a way to ask questions, and to provide any instructions for the attendees.

8   In the Chat window, type a message (such as "Welcome to the meeting") then click Send. If you have an attendee set up, you can have them enter a reply.

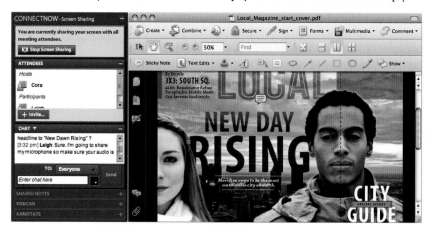

Imagine how helpful it could be if the tech person could sort out problems directly on your computer, even though the tech is only present online. That's possible with Share My Screen, because you can hand over control of your computer to another participant in the meeting.

9 In the ConnectNow screen sharing panel, click the triangle to the right of the attendee's name and choose Give This User Control Of My Computer.

Being able to work in the application that was used to create the artwork has the advantage that you or any trusted reviewer can quickly react to a suggestion. For example, it would take you only a couple of seconds to demonstrate how the cover would look with a different headline.

Note: You can use the microphone on your computer to speak with other meeting attendees using VoIP. Alternatively, use one of the conference numbers provided for traditional teleconferencing.

10 To leave the online conference, click Exit Adobe ConnectNow.

Bravo! You finished the online review and with it the last lesson in this book. You've covered a lot of ground: from creating basic assets to publishing a magazine in both printed and interactive form—from prototyping and building a website and designing for mobile devices to experimenting with different review workflows. There is so much more you can do with Adobe Creative Suite 5 Design Premium—this is just the beginning!

Troubleshooting checklist

This checklist may help if you encounter difficulties setting up or attending an online conference:

- Ensure that you are connected to the Internet.
- Check that your software and hardware meet the system requirements. For a complete list, see www.adobe.com/go/acrobatconnect_systemreqs.
- Disable any pop-up blocker software.
- Clear the browser cache.
- Try connecting from another computer.
- Ensure that you have entered the correct URL.
- Try joining the meeting as a registered user or as guest.
- Confirm that you are using the correct password.

Review questions

1 What are the advantages of the shared review using a centralized server?

2 Describe three of Acrobat's comment or markup tools, and explain where to find them.

3 Describe three ways to review a PDF file online.

Review answers

1 Using a centralized server allows all participants to collaborate directly with each other rather than only through the initiator. Not only can they read and reply to each others' comments, but they also receive notifications when new comments are published.

2 The comment and markup tools in Acrobat can be accessed by choosing View > Toolbars > Comment & Markup. These tools enable you to make edits, attach notes, and even draw diagrams to communicate your ideas or provide feedback for a PDF file being reviewed. Using the Sticky Note tool you can add your comments in the form of a yellow note icon that appears on the page with a pop-up note for your text comment. With the Text Edits tool you can make a variety of edits, such as replacing text, highlighting, underlining, or adding a note to selected text. You can insert text, or cross it out for deletion. The Stamp tool enables you to apply a stamp to a PDF in much the same way you apply a rubber stamp to a paper document. You can apply predefined stamps or stamps that you create yourself.

3 An e-mail based review lets you manage a review without a central server. A shared review lets you host a review on a central server so that reviewers can view and respond to each others' comments; with an e-mail review you're the only person who sees all of the comments. A live, collaborative review lets you and your reviewers view a document simultaneously online with the option of a chat session, while a ConnectNow meeting adds the ability to share not just one document but anything on your computer.

INDEX

Newly Expanded LEARN BY VIDEO Series

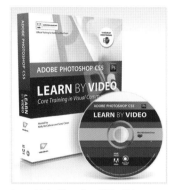

Learn Adobe Photoshop CS5 by Video:
Core Training in Visual Communication
(ISBN 9780321719805)

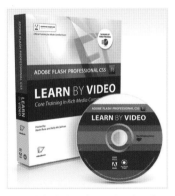

Learn Adobe Flash Professional CS5 by Video:
Core Training in Rich Media Communication
(ISBN 9780321719829)

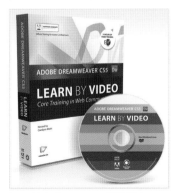

Learn Adobe Dreamweaver CS5 by Video:
Core Training in Web Communication
(ISBN 9780321719812)

The **Learn by Video** series from video2brain and Adobe Press is the only Adobe-approved video courseware for the Adobe Certified Associate Level certification, and has quickly established itself as one of the most critically-acclaimed training products available on the fundamentals of Adobe software.

Learn by Video offers up to 19 hours of high-quality HD video training presented by experienced trainers, as well as lesson files, assessment quizzes and review materials. The DVD is bundled with a full-color printed book that provides supplemental information as well as a guide to the video topics.

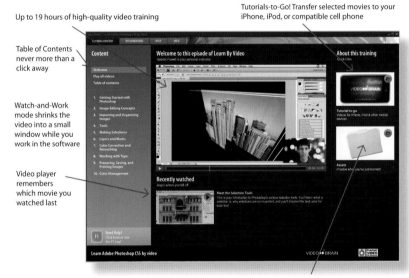

Up to 19 hours of high-quality video training

Tutorials-to-Go! Transfer selected movies to your iPhone, iPod, or compatible cell phone

Table of Contents never more than a click away

Watch-and-Work mode shrinks the video into a small window while you work in the software

Video player remembers which movie you watched last

Lesson files are included on the DVD

Additional Titles

- **Learn Adobe Photoshop Elements 8 and Adobe Premiere Elements 8 by Video** (ISBN 9780321685773)
- **Learn Photography Techniques for Adobe Photoshop CS5 by Video** (ISBN 9780321734839)
- **Learn Adobe After Effects CS5 by Video** (ISBN 9780321734860)
- **Learn Adobe Flash Catalyst CS5 by Video** (ISBN 9780321734853)
- **Learn Adobe Illustrator CS5 by Video** (ISBN 9780321734815)
- **Learn Adobe InDesign CS5 by Video** (ISBN 9780321734808)
- **Learn Adobe Premiere Pro CS5 by Video** (ISBN 9780321734846)

For more information go to **www.adobepress.com/learnbyvideo**

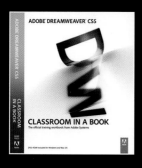
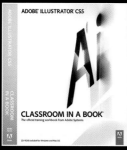
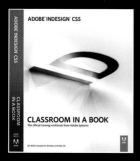

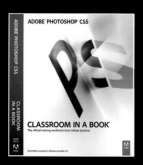

WATCH
READ
CREATE

Meet Creative Edge.

A new resource of unlimited books, videos and tutorials for creatives from the world's leading experts.

Creative Edge is your one stop for inspiration, answers to technical questions and ways to stay at the top of your game so you can focus on what you do best—being creative.

All for only $24.99 per month for access—any day any time you need it.

creativeedge.com